OTHER EARLY CHRISTIAN GOSPELS

OTHER EARLY CHRISTIAN GOSPELS

A Critical Edition of the Surviving
Greek Manuscripts

Andrew E. Bernhard

t&t clark

Published by T&T Clark
A Continuum imprint

The Tower Building   80 Maiden Lane
11 York Road   Suite 704
London SE1 7NX   New York, NY 10038

www.tandtclark.com

First published in hardback as volume 315 of the Library of New Testament studies, 2006

This edition published, 2007

British Library Cataloguing-in-Publication Data
A catalogue record for this book is available from the British Library

Typeset by RefineCatch Ltd, Bungay, Suffolk
Printed on acid-free paper in Great Britain by
Cromwell Press Ltd, Trowbridge, Wiltshire

ISBN-10: 0–567–04568–4 (paperback)
ISBN-13: 978–0–567–04568–3 (paperback)

To the memory of Gene and Brian Huntley

'Verily, verily, I say unto you, Except a corn of wheat fall into the ground and die, it abideth alone: but if it die, it bringeth forth much fruit.'

John 12.24

CONTENTS

LIST OF PLATES

ACKNOWLEDGEMENTS

When I began research for this book as a student at Willamette University in 1996, I had no idea what would be required to bring the project to completion. I never would have made it without considerable encouragement and assistance from others. I owe special thanks to the following people for their help.

Dirk Obbink and Nick Gonis, my papyrology instructors at the University of Oxford, gave me the best training and hands-on experience any graduate student could ever hope for. Robert Simpson, also of Oxford, pushed me to my limits as he taught me Coptic and patiently fielded my questions about ancient Egypt. Mark Goodacre of Duke University offered constructive criticism of drafts of portions of the book and generously shared his insights about the process of publishing a book. Thomas Kraus supplied me with vital information about ancient manuscripts and their current housing locations. Dieter Lührmann, formerly of Philipps-Universität Marburg, called my attention to recent developments in the study of early Christian gospels and helped me obtain a copy of his important book, *Fragmente apokryph gewordener Evangelien in griechischer und lateinischer Sprache*. The assistance of all these scholars was, of course, only positive; any shortcomings in this book remain my responsibility alone.

The Houghton Library at Harvard University, the University Library at the University of Cambridge, the Institut für Altertumskunde at the University of Cologne, the Bodleian Library and Centre for the Study of Ancient Documents (CSAD) at the University of Oxford, the Egypt Exploration Society (EES) and the British Library in London, and the Ägyptisches Museum und Papyrussammlung in Berlin have all generously granted me permission to publish their photographs of various manuscripts. I am most appreciative that Leslie Morris of the Houghton Library, D. J. Hall of the University Library, Robert Daniel of the Institut für Altertumskunde, Melissa Dalziel of the Bodleian Library, Alan Bowman and Charles Crowther of CSAD, Patricia Spencer of the EES, Christine Campbell of the British Library and Günter Poethke of the Ägyptisches Museum und Papyrussammlung were willing to help me secure the required permissions from their respective institutions.

John Hayton, Nick Lovell and Stefan Alexander kindly evaluated my translations and offered suggestions about how to make the book more accessible to the general reader. Roger Pearse, founder of tertullian.org, helped me greatly by forcing me to clarify my ideas and statements about early Christian gospels. Craig Riley persevered through a complete draft of the book to ensure that it was sufficiently polished. Sarah Gibbs devoted untold time and energy to reading drafts and tracking down information.

Nathan Sasaki and Murin Lesewski contributed more to the successful completion of this book than they will ever know. I am exceedingly grateful that they have been willing to show me the ropes. Steve Kong also provided important advice about the book project. Rebecca Vaughan-Williams has been exceptional in her role as an editor at T&T Clark International. The importance of her professionalism and diligence in helping me prepare the book for publication cannot be overstated.

I am especially indebted to the Department of Religious Studies at Willamette University. In particular, Doug McGaughey and Lane McGaughy have far exceeded their duties as my professors. They have ceaselessly and selflessly helped me with my research, and each has showed me by his example what it means to be a good human being. If all the things that they have done to help me were written out one by one, I suppose that even the world itself could not contain the books that should be written.

Finally, I am most grateful for the unfailing support of my family. Without it, I would not have had the opportunity to undertake this project, let alone complete it. Thank you, Grandma Huntley, Ted, James, Dianna, Cassidy and Caitlyn, for lifting me up and giving meaning to my life. Thank you, Mom and Dad, for unconditional love.

ABBREVIATIONS

Bibliographical

Aeg	*Aegyptus*
BASP	*Bulletin of the American Society of Papyrologists*
BASPSup	Bulletin of the American Society of Papyrologists: Supplement
ChrEg	*Chronique d'Egypte*
CRAIBL	*Comptes rendus de l'Académie des inscriptions et belles-lettres*
EvT	*Evangelische Theologie*
ExpTim	*Expository Times*
HibJ	*Hibbert Journal*
HTR	*Harvard Theological Review*
JA	*Journal asiatique*
JBL	*Journal of Biblical Literature*
JTS	*Journal of Theological Studies*
KlT	Kleine Texte für theologische und philologische Vorlesungen und Übungen
MMAF	Mémoires publiés par les membres de la Mission archéologique française au Caire
NKZ	*Neue kirchliche Zeitschrift*
NovT	*Novum Testamentum*
PO	Patrologia orientalis
REG	*Revue des études grecques*
TS	*Theological Studies*
TSK	*Theologische Studien und Kritiken*
ZAC	*Zeitschrift für Antikes Christentum*
ZKT	*Zeitschrift für katholische Theologie*
ZNW	*Zeitschrift für die neutestamentliche Wissenschaft und die Kunde der älteren Kirche*
ZWT	*Zeitschrift für wissenschaftliche Theologie*

New Testament

Mt.	Matthew
Mk	Mark
Lk.	Luke
Jn	John
2 Cor.	2 Corinthians
Phil.	Philippians
Col.	Colossians

Non-biblical ancient texts

2 Clem.	*2 Clement*
Did.	*Didache*
Gos. Pet.	*Gospel of Peter*
Gos. Thom.	*Gospel of Thomas*
Hist. eccl.	*Ecclesiastical History* by Eusebius

Organizations

EES	Egypt Exploration Society
CSAD	Centre for the Study of Ancient Documents

Papyri and other ancient manuscripts

P.Berol.	Berlin Papyrus
P.Cair.	Cairo Papyrus
P.Egerton	Egerton Papyrus
P.Köln	Cologne Papyrus
P.Mert.	Merton Papyrus
P.Oxy.	Oxyrhynchus Papyrus/Parchment
P.Ryl.	Rylands Papyrus
P.Vindob.G	Vienna Papyrus (Greek)

Other Abbreviations

ca.	circa
CE	Common Era
cf.	compare

Abbreviations

cm	centimetre
ed(s).	editor(s)
edn	edition
e.g.	for example
exp.	expanded
h.	height
i.e.	that is
lit.	literally
ms.	manuscript
p(p).	page(s)
pap.	papyrus
rev.	revised
sg.	singular
vol(s).	volume(s)
w.	width

GENERAL INTRODUCTION

Since the late nineteenth century, our knowledge of early Christianity and its literature has been significantly improved by the recovery of numerous ancient manuscripts. Professional archaeologists and others digging in the dry sands of Egypt have discovered copies of New Testament texts that are hundreds of years older than any previously known Christian manuscript.[1] They have also unearthed some remarkable papyrus and parchment manuscripts containing long-lost Christian writings that never became a part of the official canon of scripture.

Especially intriguing are the Greek manuscripts that preserve portions of little-known early Christian gospels, such as the *Gospel of Thomas*, the *Gospel of Peter* and the *Unknown Gospel* of Egerton Papyrus 2. These fragmentary manuscripts provide us with direct access to texts that seem to have been written at about the same time as the New Testament gospels. They allow us to study ancient writings about the life of Jesus in their original language, without the filters of later translation or commentary. They make long-forgotten gospels penned by some of Jesus' earliest followers available once again, shedding new light on the formative years of Christianity and, perhaps, even on Jesus himself.

A new collection of manuscripts containing early Christian gospels

The purpose of this book is to collect all the recently recovered Greek manuscripts containing parts of early Christian gospels (other than

---

1. The famous fourth-century majuscule (uncial) codices, Sinaiticus and Vaticanus, were the oldest copies of New Testament texts known to modern scholars until B. P. Grenfell and A. S. Hunt uncovered a third-century fragment of Matthew (P.Oxy. 2) at Oxyrhynchus in 1897. Since that time, more than fifty other New Testament papyri from the second and third centuries have been found. Transcriptions of all of these papyri are conveniently available in P. W. Comfort and D. P. Barrett (eds.), *The Text of the Earliest New Testament Greek Manuscripts* (Wheaton, IL.: Tyndale House Publishers, 2001).

Matthew, Mark, Luke and John) into a single volume.[2] For convenience, the term 'gospel' is used as a label for any written text that is primarily focused on recounting the teachings and/or activities of Jesus during his adult life. The designation 'early' refers to the first hundred years of the Christian movement (ca. 30–130 CE), the time period in which the four New Testament gospels were apparently written.[3]

With so much ongoing discussion about newly available early Christian gospels at the present time, a comprehensive sourcebook of the pertinent Greek manuscripts seems warranted.[4] The manuscripts (most of which are fragile papyrus fragments) are now locked away in various museums and libraries around the world. Published editions (most of which are now long out of date) are often difficult to locate because they have been released in obscure books and periodicals by different scholars at different times in different editorial languages. Amazingly, no comprehensive original language edition has ever been created for the English-speaking world.[5]

Manuscripts included in this collection

New editions of thirteen Greek manuscripts are presented in this book.[6] Seven of the manuscripts preserve portions of gospels that are widely believed to have been written before 130 CE. The other six contain small

---

2. The four early Christian gospels that became a part of the New Testament (Matthew, Mark, Luke and John) are omitted from this collection only because they are already available in innumerable editions.

3. The vast majority of scholars today believe that all four of the New Testament gospels were written between 65 and 100 CE, with Mark the earliest and John the latest. However, the 'consensus' dates for the New Testament gospels are neither universally accepted nor certain. Slightly earlier or later dates are also quite possible and are still advocated today by competent scholars.

4. S. E. Porter called for a new critical edition of 'Greek apocryphal gospel papyri' at the 21st International Congress of Papyrology in 1995, noting that discussion of a number of gospel manuscripts (P.Oxy. 1, 654, 655, 840, 1081, 1224, 2949, 4009; P.Cair. 10735, 10759; P.Egerton 2 + P.Köln 255; P.Vindob.G 2325; P.Mert. 51; P.Berol. 11710) had been significantly impaired by the lack of a satisfactory edition. See S. E. Porter, 'The Greek Apocryphal Gospels Papyri: The Need for a Critical Edition', in vol. 2 of *Akten des 21. Internationalen Papyrologenkongresses: Berlin, 13.-19.8.1995* (eds. B. Kramer, W. Luppe, H. Maehler and G. Poethke; Stuttgart: B.G. Teubner, 1997), pp. 795–803.

5. The lone attempt was J. Finegan, *Hidden Records of the Life of Jesus* (Philadelphia, PA: Pilgrim Press, 1969). This helpful volume did contain ancient language editions of some little-known gospels, but it was far from comprehensive and, unfortunately, was never updated after its initial publication.

6. P.Cair. 10735, P.Oxy. 3525, P.Ryl. 463 and P.Oxy. 1081 are not included in this collection because the texts they preserve are not 'gospels' according to the definition used in this book (i.e., the texts they preserve are not primarily about the *adult life* of Jesus). The preserved

excerpts of unidentified gospels that may or may not originally have been written during the first hundred years of the Christian movement (scholars disagree significantly about when these gospels were originally written).

The former group of manuscripts consists of the three Greek fragments of the *Gospel of Thomas* (P.Oxy. 654, 1, 655), the three fragments of the *Gospel of Peter* (P.Oxy. 4009, P.Cair. 10759, P.Oxy. 2949), and the lone manuscript of the *Unknown Gospel* (P.Egerton 2 + P.Köln 255). Although some of these manuscripts come from the middle of the third century or later, at least one surviving manuscript of each gospel can be reliably dated to the second hundred years of Christianity (ca. 130–230 CE). Thus, it is clear that the *Gospel of Thomas*, *Gospel of Peter* and *Unknown Gospel* circulated, like the New Testament gospels, in second-century Christian communities (see Table 1).[7]

Internal characteristics of the texts suggest that the *Gospel of Thomas*, *Gospel of Peter* and *Unknown Gospel* were most likely written during the first hundred years or so of the Christian movement, some time before the New Testament gospels attained pre-eminence in the mid-second century. These three recently recovered gospels include stories and sayings that are known to have circulated in early Christian communities, but they lack passages that are demonstrably dependent on the New Testament gospels[8] and seem to preserve some early traditions about Jesus in a more primitive form than Matthew, Mark, Luke or John.[9] Furthermore, these newly

portions of the unidentified text found on P.Cair. 10735 deal exclusively with the infancy of Jesus. The *Gospel of Mary* (P.Oxy. 3525, P.Ryl. 463) and the *Sophia of Jesus Christ* (P.Oxy. 1081) deal exclusively with post-resurrection events.

7. It is impossible to know how popular the *Gospel of Thomas*, *Gospel of Peter* and *Unknown Gospel* were in the second century. They are surprisingly well attested among our most ancient Christian manuscripts, as noted in H. Koester, 'Apocryphal and Canonical Gospels', *HTR* 73 (1980), pp. 105–30 (107–10). However, the few gospel manuscripts from 130–230 CE that have been preserved (purely by chance) in one geographic location (Egypt) may not provide a representative sample of all the gospel manuscripts that existed during this time period.

8. The *Gospel of Thomas*, *Gospel of Peter* and *Unknown Gospel* have obvious parallels with the New Testament gospels, but they do not exhibit the kind of pattern of extensive verbal correspondence with any of the New Testament texts that would be necessary to establish direct literary dependence. For the most part, the observed parallels are understood well as the result of common oral traditions, shared written sources and/or the harmonization of originally independent texts by later scribes.

9. For example, the *Gospel of Thomas* lacks the allegorical additions of the New Testament gospels in its version of the Parable of the Sower (*Gos. Thom.* 9; Mt. 13.3–23; Mk 4.2–20; Lk. 8.4–15) and its version of the Parable of the Tenants (*Gos. Thom.* 65; Mt. 21.33–39; Mk 12.1–8; Lk. 20.9–15). See M. Meyer, *The Gospel of Thomas: The Hidden Sayings of Jesus* (San Francisco, CA: HarperSanFrancisco, 1992), pp. 13–14; J. S. Kloppenborg, M. Meyer, S. J. Patterson and M. G. Steinhauser, *Q-Thomas Reader* (Sonoma, CA.: Polebridge Press,

Table 1. Gospel manuscripts (ca. 130–230 CE)	
Gospel	*Manuscript (approximate date)*
Matthew	𝔓104 (second century)
	𝔓64+𝔓67 (late second/early third century)†
	𝔓77+𝔓103 (late second/early third century)
John	𝔓52 (second century)‡
	𝔓90 (second century)
	𝔓66 (late second/early third century)
Gospel of Peter	P.Oxy. 4009 (second century)
	P.Oxy. 2949 (late second/early third century)
Unknown Gospel	P.Egerton 2 + P.Köln 255 (second century)
Luke	𝔓4 (late second/early third century)†
Gospel of Thomas	P.Oxy. 1 (late second/early third century)
Mark	None extant

† 𝔓4, 𝔓64 and 𝔓67 may all be part of the same manuscript.
‡ 𝔓52 could be slightly earlier than 130 CE. It is usually dated ca. 125 CE.

available gospels give no indication that they were written after 130 CE: they never refer to any known historical event after this time, nor do they ever allude to any peculiarly second-century Christian beliefs.

The six other manuscripts presented in this book (P.Vindob.G 2325, P.Mert. 51, P.Oxy. 210, P.Oxy. 1224, P.Oxy. 840, P.Berol. 11710) are small fragments of various unidentified gospels. All six different texts known from these badly damaged manuscripts can reasonably be regarded as early Christian gospels, but it should be noted that they cannot be dated precisely. For example, one unidentified gospel is known only from a single manuscript that comes from the fourth century (P.Oxy. 840). The gospel itself might originally have been written during the first century, as some scholars suggest.[10] Or, it might have been written in the second or third century, as

1990), p. 102. The *Gospel of Peter* seems to cite passages from the Hebrew Bible in a more primitive manner than the New Testament gospels do. See P. Vielhauer, *Geschichte der urchristlichen Literatur: Einleitung in das Neue Testament, die Apokryphen und die Apostolischen Väter* (Berlin: Walter de Gruyter, 1975), p. 646. The version of the dispute between Jesus and the Jewish leaders in fragment 1(↓).7–23 of the *Unknown Gospel,* is unquestionably more original than the version in Jn 5.39–46 (and 9.29). See especially H. Koester, *Ancient Christian Gospels: Their History and Development* (Philadelphia, PA: Trinity Press International, 1990), pp. 208–10.

10. See, for example, K. Berger and C. Nord, *Das Neue Testament und frühchristliche Schriften* (Leipzig: Insel Verlag, 1999), p. 299.

others argue.[11] Whatever the case, the manuscript of this gospel and five other manuscripts like it are included here because it has seemed best not to exclude any *possible* early Christian gospels.

Structure of the collection

This book is divided into four chapters. The first chapter is devoted to the Greek fragments of the *Gospel of Thomas*, the second to the *Gospel of Peter*, the third to the *Unknown Gospel* and the fourth to the other unidentified gospel fragments. Chapters contain the following sections: introduction, manuscript notes, critical Greek text, student's Greek text and English translation. The book concludes with exhaustive indexes for the critical Greek texts, an index of biblical citations, an index of modern authors and plates for most of the manuscripts.

Introductions

Each chapter begins with a brief introduction about the gospel (or group of gospels) that is the subject of the chapter. The introductions are limited to the basic facts that are known about the gospels, such as how they were recovered in modern times and what material they contain. The introductions are not intended to provide commentary on the contents of the gospels. They do not advocate a particular position on matters of scholarly debate, such as what the theological intentions of the author were or precisely when and where the texts were originally written. Such interpretive issues are beyond the scope of this sourcebook.

Manuscript notes

The manuscript notes that follow every introduction provide information about the manuscripts presented in the chapter that could not be effectively included within the Greek texts themselves. The notes offer a basic description of the physical characteristics of each manuscript and indicate where each manuscript is currently housed. They also include select bibliographies that detail the most important published editions of each manuscript.

The bibliographies include three primary types of entries. The 'first published edition' is simply the first edition of a manuscript released to the

---

11. See, for example, the extended argument in F. Bovon, 'Fragment Oxyrhynchus 840, Fragment of a Lost Gospel, Witness of an Early Christian Controversy over Purity', *JBL* 119 (2000), pp. 705–28.

public in print, regardless of its format (i.e., whether it is a book, book section or periodical article). The 'official publication' is the edition of a manuscript published in a series of books created specifically to make manuscripts from a particular collection available in a uniform format (e.g., any edition included in a volume of the *Oxyrhynchus Papyri*). A 'critical edition' is an edition that compiles scholarly notes from a number of other editions. Other especially important editions are also noted in the bibliographies on occasion.

Presentation of the texts

After the manuscript notes, three different versions of the manuscripts are presented using facing pages to facilitate easy access for scholars, students and laypeople. The left-hand page is always occupied completely by the critical Greek text; this version presents the Greek text along with the editorial signs and apparatus necessary for in-depth scholarly analysis. The right-hand page always contains an English translation; all translations are intended to be as transparent to their underlying Greek texts as smooth, contemporary, idiomatic English will allow.[12] The right-hand page also contains a student's Greek text for many of the more fragmentary manuscripts; this version presents the restored Greek text without the potentially confusing apparatus, editorial signs and unidentifiable word fragments found in the critical version.

Indexes

The Greek indexes that appear after the final chapter record all appearances of every word found in the critical Greek texts, with the exceptions of the definite article and the common conjunction καί. The words found in the three fragments of the *Gospel of Thomas* are presented in a single index. All other manuscripts have been indexed individually. Words that have been restored, either fully or in part, are indicated by an asterisk. Words appearing uniquely in the apparatus are indicated by a superscript 'ap'.

---

12.   Strictly literal translations have been adopted whenever possible, but minor refinements have occasionally been necessary to ensure that translations always obey the conventions of English grammar, word order and sense. The vast majority of the stylistic adjustments that have been made involve the use of καί and δέ at the beginnings of sentences or the redundant use of a participial form of ἀποκρίνομαι with another verb of speaking (e.g., λέγω, εἶπον, φημί).

The two remaining indexes are straightforward. The first catalogues all the biblical citations that appear in this book. The second lists the modern authors whose works are mentioned herein.

Plates

The plates at the end of the book present photographs of all the Greek fragments of the *Gospel of Thomas* (P.Oxy. 654, 1, 655), the *Gospel of Peter* (P.Oxy. 4009, P.Cair. 10759, P.Oxy. 2949), and the *Unknown Gospel* (P.Egerton 2 + P.Köln 255). In addition, the plates include previously unpublished photographs of P.Oxy. 210, fragments 1($\downarrow$) and 2($\rightarrow$) of P.Oxy. 1224, the back of P.Oxy. 840[13] and P.Berol. 11710.[14] All the manuscripts are shown at actual size in the photographs, with the exception of P.Oxy. 654 which has been reduced to 70 per cent of actual size so that it can be shown in its entirety on a single page.

---

13. After the initial manuscript of this book was completed, photographs of the back (and front) of P.Oxy. 840 were published in M. J. Kruger, *The Gospel of the Savior: An Analysis of P. Oxy. 840 and its Place in the Gospel Traditions of Early Christianity* (eds. S. E. Porter and W. J. Porter; Texts and Editions for New Testament Study, 1; Leiden: Brill, 2005).

14. With the release of this book, photographs of all parts of all the manuscripts under consideration here are now available in published form. Photographs of the parts of P.Vindob.G 2325, P.Mert. 51, P.Oxy. 1224 and P.Oxy. 840 that are not presented here are readily available in the publications listed in the manuscript notes.

EDITORIAL METHOD

The critical Greek texts occupy a central position in this book not only because they are important scholarly tools in their own right, but also because they are the basis for the English translations and the student's Greek texts. Since the critical Greek texts are so important here and differ in some respects from other editions of ancient manuscripts, it seems best to state the principles on which they are based.

Textual divisions

The critical Greek texts are divided into sections. For the *Gospel of Thomas* and the *Gospel of Peter*, the established textual divisions have been used. The three fragments of the *Gospel of Thomas* (P.Oxy. 654, 1, 655) are divided into sayings. The Akhmim fragment of the *Gospel of Peter* (P.Cair. 10759) is divided into chapters (and verses indicated by italic Arabic numerals within the text). For all other manuscripts, the critical Greek texts have been divided into sections on the basis of natural manuscript divisions, such as the start of a new page or column.

At the beginning of each section, the precise location where the text can be found on an ancient manuscript is stated. In referring to the different sides of papyri, the side on which the fibres run horizontally is designated (→); the side on which the fibres run vertically is designated (↓).[1] The terms 'recto' and 'verso' have not been used because their value now seems irretrievably lost.[2]

One line of critical Greek text always corresponds to exactly one line of Greek text read on an ancient manuscript. For P.Oxy. 840 and P.Berol.

---

1. Fibre direction is, of course, the direction the fibres run when the text on the papyrus is held in the upright position (i.e., horizontal fibres run parallel to lines of text and vertical fibres run perpendicular to them).

2. For a complete discussion of the problems associated with using the terms 'recto' and 'verso' in papyrology, see E. G. Turner, *The Terms Recto and Verso; The Anatomy of the Papyrus Roll* (Brussels: Fondation égyptologique Reine Élisabeth, 1978).

11710, the established line numbering has been retained so that lines of text appearing on consecutive pages are numbered continuously.[3] For all other manuscripts, the first line of each column of text is treated as line 1.[4]

Greek text

The critical Greek texts themselves are based on a recollation of the ancient manuscripts. All readings have been checked against a high-quality photograph and against the transcriptions of other editors who had manuscript access. In every possible instance, the manuscript itself has also been consulted.[5] The original editors of the manuscripts have been given the benefit of the doubt with readings that could be neither confirmed nor discredited, especially when the readings involved text near the edge of a manuscript.

Corrupt text has been corrected for the sake of readability, but all editorial corrections that have been made are noted in the apparatus. In addition, accents, breathing marks, iota subscripts and punctuation not present on the ancient manuscripts have been added. Spaces have been inserted between words, and the first letters of proper names have been capitalized. All such features that appear in the critical Greek texts should be regarded as purely modern additions. Original features of this kind are noted in the apparatus or manuscript notes.

Given the fragmentary nature of many of the manuscripts, it has frequently been necessary to restore damaged and lost text. Three primary types of restorations are offered.

Restorations based on context

Some small restorations are required because of the limited lexical, morphological and syntactical possibilities allowed by preserved text. For instance, the preserved text at the right edge of line 14 of P.Oxy. 654 reads, οι ιχθυες της θαλα; the final four letters of θαλα[σσης] must obviously be restored. Such restorations are virtually certain.

---

3. There is no harm in maintaining the traditional continuous line numbering with P.Oxy. 840 and P.Berol. 11710 because all the lines of text on these manuscripts are unquestionably consecutive (i.e., the top and bottom margins are still visible).

4. Continuous line numbering can be misleading when the top and/or bottom margins (and an uncertain number of lines of text near these margins) have been lost; it becomes especially problematic when additional pieces of a manuscript are recovered, as with P.Egerton 2.

5. The present editor has had the privilege of viewing the following manuscripts: P.Oxy. 654, P.Oxy. 1, P.Oxy. 2949, P.Oxy. 4009, P.Egerton 2, P.Oxy. 210, P.Oxy. 1224 and P.Oxy. 840.

Restorations based on convincing parallels

Some proposed restorations are based on parallels in other known texts, usually the New Testament gospels. Using one text to reconstruct another is admittedly not ideal, but it does enable the general sense of many damaged passages to be restored with a reasonable degree of certainty.

Restorations based on another manuscript

The complete Coptic version of the *Gospel of Thomas* (Nag Hammadi II,2) has served as a guide for the restoration of the Greek fragments (P.Oxy. 654, 1, 655). Although the Coptic sometimes differs substantively from the Greek texts, it still provides much needed external controls.[6] Similarly, P.Cair. 10759 has served as a guide for restoring text from the *Gospel of Peter* on P.Oxy. 2949.

To restore lost text on a particular manuscript, typical letters from the preserved portion of the manuscript were copied and pasted electronically into the space of each lacuna. In arranging letters in lacunae, particular attention was paid to variations in letter spacing and margins on the manuscript.

Lacunae that could not be restored on the basis of context, other manuscripts or parallels have generally been left blank. Suggested restorations that are purely hypothetical have been omitted (regardless of the number of modern editions in which they have been printed). On rare occasions, up to three consecutive words have been supplied purely to improve the readability of a badly fragmented portion of text. Although nobody could feel confident that such restorations are actually correct, they are not misleading and serve a definite purpose.

Editorial signs

Restored text and other noteworthy textual features are indicated by the editorial signs. Square brackets [ ] indicate a lacuna, enclosing what is

---

6. The dangers of restoring lost portions of fragmentary manuscripts without external controls are illustrated well by the edition of two of the Greek fragments of the *Gospel of Thomas* found in H. G. Evelyn-White, *The Sayings of Jesus from Oxyrhynchus* (Cambridge: Cambridge University Press, 1920). Drawing on the best scholarship from 1897–1920, Evelyn-White created a critical edition of P.Oxy. 654 and P.Oxy. 1 (without P.Oxy. 655 because he mistakenly believed that it preserved part of a different gospel). Virtually all of the text restored by Evelyn-White on P.Oxy. 654 without parallels (26 of 42 lines: 1–4, 9–12, 14, 17–24, 26, 35–42) had to be discarded after the discovery of a complete Coptic version of the *Gospel of Thomas* at Nag Hammadi. Particularly misleading were his restorations of line 2, which obscured the identity of the text, and line 9, which attributed a saying of Jesus to Judas.

lacking from the manuscript. When no satisfactory restoration is available for a lacuna at the edge of the manuscript, the space is left blank and the square bracket at the margin is omitted. A dot appears beneath each letter that is uncertain: e.g., α̣. High strokes ˋ ˊ indicate a scribal insertion above the line. Editorial corrections in the form of letters to be deleted are enclosed by braces { }; letters to be added are enclosed by pointed brackets < >. Parentheses ( ) are used to indicate the expansion of an abbreviation: e.g., ιη̅ς on a manuscript appears as Ἰη(σοῦ)ς in the critical text.[7]

Pointed half-brackets ⌐ ¬ have been adapted for use from *Novum Testamentum Graece*, where they enclose text for which variant readings have been preserved on different ancient manuscripts.[8] In this book, pointed half-brackets enclose text for which substantively different and equally plausible readings or restorations of a single manuscript have been proposed by modern scholars. Substantively different readings and restorations are those that would affect the meaning of a passage and/or alter our understanding of relationships between different texts.

Apparatus

The apparatus appears at the bottom of each page of critical Greek text. Sections of the apparatus begin with a label printed in italic, which corresponds to the label of a section in the text above. Before the first entry dealing with text contained in a line (or verse for P.Cair. 10759), the line (or verse) number is printed in normal type.[9] Each entry is introduced in the apparatus by reprinting the text under consideration, either in full if it is less than six words or in part if it is longer.

---

7. The editorial signs mentioned in this paragraph are standard in modern editions of papyri. Their use has effectively been mandatory since they were recommended by the 1931 Leiden convention of papyrologists. See M. Hombert and B. A. van Groningen, 'Essai d'unification des méthodes employées dans les éditions de papyrus', *ChrEg* 7 (1932), pp. 285–87.

8. K. Aland, B. Aland, J. Karavidopoulos, C. M. Martini and B. M. Metzger (eds.), *Novum Testamentum Graece* (Stuttgart: Deutsche Bibelgesellschaft, 27th rev. edn, 1993), p. 52.

9. Although each line of critical Greek text of P.Cair. 10759 corresponds to one line on the manuscript, line numbers are not used for referencing the text because the gospel's chapter and verse numbers are adequate for this task.

apparatus:	7 41 ὁ λέων ἔσται ἄνθρωπος καὶ
meaning:	The entry pertains to text found in Saying 7 (of the *Gospel of Thomas*), beginning with ὁ in line 41 and continuing straight through to καὶ.
apparatus:	(→) 5 γίνου δὲ . . . (19) δυναμένων μηδέν
meaning:	The entry pertains to text found on the side of the papyrus with horizontal fibres, beginning with γίνου δὲ in line 5 and continuing straight through to δυναμένων μηδέν in line 19.

The apparatus contains the following four types of entries.

Attributions

All non-obvious restorations enclosed in square brackets [ ] in the critical Greek text are attributed to the scholar(s) who first proposed them in print. If the adopted restoration is a modified version of one or two earlier proposals, the other suggested restoration(s) appear. A colon is always used to separate textual variants of equal status in the apparatus.

apparatus:	ἐν ὁράματι Grenfell-Hunt[1914]
meaning:	The restoration adopted in the critical text, ἐν ὁράματι, was first proposed in a 1914 publication by Grenfell and Hunt.
apparatus:	εὑρίσκῃ Fitzmyer[1959] : εὕρῃ Puech[1957]
meaning:	The restoration adopted in the critical text, εὑρίσκῃ, was originally proposed in a 1959 publication by Fitzmyer; however, a similar restoration, εὕρῃ, was proposed in a 1957 publication by Puech.

It should be noted that attributions pertain exclusively to restored text. Attributions should not be construed as attributions of preserved text (which is visible for all to see) to a particular modern scholar, nor should they be taken as a report of non-textual features (e.g., annotation, punctuation, line divisions) presented in the cited sources. See the bibliography for information about the publication in which a suggested restoration was initially made.

apparatus:	1 πᾶς ὁ . . . (4) Φαρισαῖοι οὐκ Rees[1959]
meaning:	Rees proposed all restored text between πᾶς ὁ in line 1 and Φαρισαῖοι οὐκ in line 4 (including πᾶς ὁ and Φαρισαῖοι οὐκ, if they are restorations). For his complete presentation of the text, see the 1959 publication listed under his name in the bibliography.
apparatus:	ἠδύναντο Bell-Skeat[1935b] : ἐδύναντο Bell-Skeat[1935a]
meaning:	Bell and Skeat initially proposed the restoration ἠδύναντο in the second 1935 publication listed under their names in the bibliography (*New Gospel Fragments*); they initially proposed the restoration ἐδύναντο in the first 1935 publication listed under their names in the bibliography (*Fragments of an Unknown Gospel*).

Alternative readings/restorations

All substantively different and equally plausible readings and restorations for text enclosed by pointed half-brackets ⌐ ¬ in the critical Greek text appear in the apparatus.

apparatus:	τοῦ Πέτρου Bickell[1885] : ἐμοῦ Πέτρου Lührmann[1993]
meaning:	The restoration adopted in the critical text, τοῦ Πέτρου, was proposed in an 1885 publication by Bickell, but a substantively different and equally plausible restoration, ἐμοῦ Πέτρου, was proposed in a 1993 publication by Lührmann.

Unemended readings

For all text that has been emended in the critical Greek text, the actual reading of the manuscript is noted in the apparatus.

apparatus:	τεθαμμένον : θεθαμμενον pap.
meaning:	The text adopted in the critical text, τεθαμμένον, is an emended form of the corrupt text read on the manuscript, θεθαμμενον.
note:	pap. is used as an abbreviation for papyrus; all other types of manuscripts are designated with the abbreviation ms.

Paleographic notes

A transcription is included in the apparatus for all text with notable paleographic features on the original manuscript.

apparatus:	ὕδωρ : ὕδωρ pap.
meaning:	The word ὕδωρ in the critical text is read ὕδωρ on the papyrus (i.e., the initial upsilon has the mark of diaeresis).

In general, editorial signs and punctuation have been omitted from the apparatus. They are only included to convey important but otherwise inexpressible information. Individual entries are separated from each other in the apparatus by a double vertical line ‖.

EDITORIAL SIGNS

[ ]	lacuna in the manuscript
[α α α]	modern editor's suggested restoration for lacuna
[. . .]	lacuna wide enough to contain three standard letters
. . .	traces of three unidentified letters
α̣ α̣ α̣	paleographically ambiguous letter traces
`\ /`	text printed above the line by ancient scribe
{ }	text deleted by modern editor
( )	text added by modern editor to resolve an abbreviation
< >	text added by modern editor for any other reason
⸌ ⸍	text that could be read or restored differently; see apparatus

THE GOSPEL OF THOMAS

The modern study of the *Gospel of Thomas* began in 1897 at the site of ancient Oxyrhynchus in Egypt.[1] Bernard Grenfell and Arthur Hunt had just begun their first excavation of the city's long-undisturbed rubbish heaps when they turned up a papyrus leaf containing a portion of an unfamiliar gospel (P.Oxy. 1).[2] Fascinated by the unidentifiable gospel fragment, they promptly published an edition of it under the descriptive title, *Logia Iēsou* ('Sayings of Jesus').[3] Little did they know that they would isolate two additional fragments of the same mysterious gospel during their next excavation at the site six years later, the so-called 'New Sayings of Jesus' (P.Oxy. 654) and a 'Fragment of a Lost Gospel' (P.Oxy. 655).

Although considerable scholarly discussion followed the initial publication of the three new-found papyrus manuscripts, no consensus emerged about the identity of the text they contained. Certain identification only

---

1. Oxyrhynchus, which once stood 120 miles south of Cairo at the site of present-day el-Bahnasa, was an important centre for Christianity in Roman Egypt. For a history of Oxrhynchus from the first to seventh century CE, see H. MacLennan, *Oxyrhynchus: An Economic and Social Study* (Chicago, IL: Argonaut, Inc., Publishers, 1967). For a history of Christianity in ancient Oxrhynchus, see E. J. Epp, 'The Oxyrhynchus New Testament Papyri: "Not without Honor Except in Their Hometown"?', *JBL* 123 (2004), pp. 5–55.

2. Grenfell and Hunt led six excavations of the rubbish heaps of Oxyrhynchus between 1897 and 1907. For a first-hand account of the inital excavation, see B. P. Grenfell, 'The Oldest Record of Christ's Life: The First Complete Account of the Recent Finding of the "Sayings of Our Lord"', *McClure's Magazine* (October 1897), pp. 1022–30. For a summary of the excavations, see E. G. Turner, 'The Graeco-Roman Branch', in *Excavating in Egypt: The Egypt Exploration Society 1882–1982* (ed. T. G. H. James; Chicago: University of Chicago Press, 1982), pp. 161–78.

3. As a result of Grenfell and Hunt's original title for P.Oxy. 1, the sayings of the *Gospel of Thomas* are still sometimes referred to as *logia* (sg. *logion*). However, this terminology should be avoided because the opening line of P.Oxy. 654 describes the sayings as *logoi*, not *logia*. See W. Lock and W. Sanday, *Two Lectures on the "Sayings of Jesus" Recently Discovered at Oxyrhynchus* (Oxford: Clarendon Press, 1897), p. 16; K. Lake, 'The New Sayings of Jesus and the Synoptic Problem', *HibJ* 3 (1904–1905), pp. 332–41 (332–33); J. A. Fitzmyer, 'The Oxyrhynchus *Logoi* of Jesus and the Coptic Gospel According to Thomas', *TS* 20 (1959), pp. 505–60 (513–14).

became possible in the mid-twentieth century after an Egyptian peasant accidentally unearthed an ancient jar buried near the modern-day village of Nag Hammadi.[4] The jar yielded more than fifty fourth-century manuscripts, mostly bound up in twelve books. The second book of this 'Nag Hammadi Library' contained a complete Coptic translation of the writing that Grenfell and Hunt had partially recovered half a century earlier. The Coptic text retained its ancient title: *The Gospel According to Thomas*.

Unlike the New Testament gospels (or the similarly named *Infancy Gospel of Thomas*), the *Gospel of Thomas* known from Oxyrhynchus and Nag Hammadi is not a narrative gospel.[5] Instead, it is a sayings gospel. In it, the focus is generally not on the actions of Jesus but on his words. Although brief stories and questions occasionally prompt the statements of Jesus, his teachings are usually introduced with only the simple formula, 'Jesus said' (λέγει Ἰησοῦς). Some of the sayings seem familiar as a result of New Testament parallels; others seem peculiar because they have not been preserved in any other ancient Christian source.

On the basis of the Coptic text from Nag Hammadi, scholars have divided the *Gospel of Thomas* into a prologue and 114 sayings. The three Greek fragments preserve significant portions of the prologue and sayings 1–7, 26–33, 36–37, 39 and 77b, although they do not correspond exactly with the wording or arrangement of the Coptic version. Badly damaged portions of one of the papyri (P.Oxy. 655) may also preserve traces of sayings 24 and 38.[6]

Oxyrhynchus Papyrus 654 (P.Oxy. 654)

Contents: Gos. Thom. Prologue + 1–7 (see 'Basic description' for information about non-gospel writing on the papyrus).

4. The jar was buried only a few miles from the ancient cities of Chenoboskia and Pabau, both of which had significant ties to Pachomian monasticism. This has fuelled speculation that the manuscripts found in the jar might have originally been produced in a near-by Pachomian monastery. See J. M. Robinson (ed.), *The Nag Hammadi Library in English* (San Francisco, CA: HarperSanFrancisco, 3rd rev. edn, 1990), pp. 16–17. For a thorough narrative about the discovery of the Nag Hammadi Library, see J. Dart and R. Reigert, *Unearthing the Lost Words of Jesus* (Berkeley, CA: Seastone, 1998).

5. Substantially different versions of the *Gospel of Thomas*, and perhaps even completely different texts with the same title, may have circulated in antiquity. For the pertinent patristic references, see H. W. Attridge, 'The Greek Fragments', in vol. 1 of *Nag Hammadi Codex II, 2–7 Together with XIII, 2*, Brit. Lib. Or.4926(1), and P.Oxy. 1, 654, 655* (ed. B. Layton; Leiden: Brill, 1989), pp. 95–128 (103–09).

6. P.Oxy. 655, fragment d preserves portions of two Greek words (φωτεινῷ and κόσμῳ) that are apparently found in Coptic translation in the Nag Hammadi version of saying 24. The few letters that can be read at the top of the second column preserved by fragments a–c (lines 2–11) are often thought to be a part of saying 38 because the almost completely lost text would have appeared between sayings 37 and 39.

Date copied: Middle or late third century (Grenfell and Hunt).

Basic description: Papyrus roll; one fragment, w. 7.8 x h. 24.4 cm; 42 partially preserved lines of gospel text on the side with vertical fibres (↓); land survey preserved on the side with horizontal fibres (→).

Nomina sacra: ιης ('Ιησοῦς).

Other notable features: Text divided using paragraphus signs, in the form of a horizontal rule (——), and the coronis (⟩).

Current housing location: British Library, London.

Museum ID: Papyrus 1531.

First published edition: B. P. Grenfell and A. S. Hunt, *New Sayings of Jesus and Fragment of a Lost Gospel from Oxyrhynchus* (London: Oxford University Press, 1904).

Official publication + colour manuscript photos: B. P. Grenfell and A. S. Hunt, '654. New Sayings of Jesus', in vol. 4 of *The Oxyrhynchus Papyri* (London: Egypt Exploration Fund, 1904), pp. 1–22.

Oxyrhynchus Papyrus 1 *(P.Oxy. 1)*

Contents: Gos. Thom. 26–30, 77b, 31–33.

Date copied: Late second or early third century (Grenfell and Hunt).

Basic description: Papyrus codex; most of one leaf, w. 9.5 x h. 14.5 cm; 42 mostly preserved lines of text.

Nomina sacra: ανων (ἀνθρώπων); θυ (θεοῦ); ις ('Ιησοῦς); πρα (πατέρα); πριδι (πατρίδι).

Other notable features: Side with vertical fibres (↓) labelled page ια (11) by a later hand; 7-shaped sign (7) appears at the end of a few lines on the side with vertical fibres (↓), apparently to give all the lines an appearance of even length; some final nus suppressed, indicated by a supralinear stroke over the preceding letter.

Current housing location: Bodleian Library, University of Oxford.

Museum ID: MS. Gr. Th. e. 7 (P).

First published edition: B. P. Grenfell and A. S. Hunt, *ΛΟΓΙΑ ΙΗΣΟΥ: Sayings of Our Lord from an Early Greek Papyrus* (London: Henry Frowde, 1897).

Official publication: B. P. Grenfell and A. S. Hunt, '1. ΛΟΓΙΑ ΙΗΣΟΥ', in vol. 1 of *The Oxyrhynchus Papyri* (London: Egypt Exploration Fund, 1898), pp. 1–3.

Oxyrhynchus Papyrus 655 *(P.Oxy. 655)*

Contents: Gos. Thom. 24(?), 36–37, 38(?), 39.

Date copied: Third century (Grenfell and Hunt).

Basic description: Papyrus roll; eight fragments, w. 3.2 x h. 6.2 cm (fragment a), w. 8.3 x h. 8.2 cm (fragment b), w. 1.7 x h. 6.0 cm (fragment c), w. 3.1 x h. 3.7 cm (fragment d), tiny (fragments e–h); 48 partially preserved lines of text + space for 3 more that have been completely lost.

Nomina sacra: None visible.

Current housing location: Houghton Library, Harvard University.

Museum ID: SM Inv. 4367.

First published edition: B. P. Grenfell and A. S. Hunt, *New Sayings of Jesus and Fragment of a Lost Gospel from Oxyrhynchus* (London: Oxford University Press, 1904).

Official publication + colour manuscript photos: B. P. Grenfell and A. S. Hunt, '655. Fragment of a Lost Gospel', in vol. 4 of *The Oxyrhynchus Papyri* (London: Egypt Exploration Fund, 1904), pp. 22–28.

Other important editions

Pre-Nag Hammadi critical edition (P.Oxy. 654, 1 only): H. G. Evelyn-White, *The Sayings of Jesus from Oxyrhynchus* (Cambridge: Cambridge University Press, 1920).

Post-Nag Hammadi edition with textual commentary: J. A. Fitzmyer, 'The Oxyrhynchus *Logoi* of Jesus and the Coptic Gospel According to Thomas', *TS* 20 (1959), pp. 505–60.

Revision of post-Nag Hammadi edition with textual commentary: J. A. Fitzmyer, *Essays on the Semitic Background of the New Testament* (London: Geoffrey Chapman, 1971).

Post-Nag Hammadi edition with Greek retranslation of Coptic text: R. Kasser, *L'Évangile selon Thomas: Présentation et commentaire théologique* (Neuchatel, Switzerland: Delachaux & Niestlé, 1961).

Post-Nag Hammadi critical Greek edition: H. W. Attridge, 'The Greek Fragments', in vol. 1 of *Nag Hammadi Codex II, 2–7 Together with XIII, 2*, Brit. Lib. Or.4926(1), and P.Oxy. 1, 654, 655* (ed. B. Layton; Leiden: Brill, 1989), pp. 95–128.

Prologue

P.Oxy. 654(↓), lines 1–3

1 οὗτοι οἱ λόγοι οἱ [ἀπόκρυφοι οὓς ἐλά-]
2 λησεν Ἰη(σοῦ)ς ὁ ζῶν κ[αὶ ἔγραψεν Ἰούδα<ς> ὁ]
3 καὶ Θωμᾶ<ς>.

Saying 1

P.Oxy. 654(↓), lines 3–5

3   καὶ εἶπεν· [ὅστις ἂν τὴν ἑρμηνεί-]
4 αν τῶν λόγων τούτ[ων εὑρίσκῃ, θανάτου]
5 οὐ μὴ γεύσηται. ⤜

Prologue 1 οὗτοι οἱ Swete[1904] : {οἱ} τοῖοι οἱ Grenfell-Hunt[1904a] : οιτοιοιοι pap. ‖ ἀπόκρυφοι Zahn[1905] ‖ οὓς ἐλάλησεν Grenfell-Hunt[1904a] ‖ 2 καὶ ἔγραψεν Puech[1957] ‖ Ἰούδα<ς> ὁ καὶ Θωμᾶ<ς> : Ἰούδα(ς) ὁ καὶ Θωμᾶ(ς) Puech[1957] : Ἰούδᾳ τῷ καὶ Θωμᾷ Lake (cited in Grenfell-Hunt[1904a])
1 3 ὅστις ἂν Fitzmyer[1959] : ὃς ἂν Puech[1957] ‖ τὴν ἑρμηνείαν Puech[1957] ‖ 4 τούτων Grenfell-Hunt[1904a] ‖ εὑρίσκῃ Fitzmyer[1959] : εὕρῃ Puech[1957] ‖ θανάτου Grenfell-Hunt[1904a]

Prologue οὗτοι οἱ λόγοι οἱ ἀπόκρυφοι οὓς ἐλάλησεν Ἰησοῦς ὁ ζῶν καὶ ἔγραψεν Ἰούδας ὁ καὶ Θωμᾶς.

These are the secret sayings that the living Jesus spoke and Judas, who is also called Thomas, wrote down.

1 καὶ εἶπεν· ὅστις ἂν τὴν ἑρμηνείαν τῶν λόγων τούτων εὑρίσκῃ, θανάτου οὐ μὴ γεύσηται.

And he said, 'Whoever finds the interpretation of these sayings will not taste death.'

Saying 2

P.Oxy. 654(↓), lines 5–9

5   [λέγει Ἰη(σοῦ)ς·
6   μὴ παυσάσθω ὁ ζη[τῶν τοῦ ζητεῖν ἕως ἂν]
7   εὕρῃ, καὶ ὅταν εὕρῃ [θαμβηθήσεται, καὶ θαμ-]
8   βηθεὶς βασιλεύσει, κα[ὶ βασιλεύσας ἀναπα-]
9   ήσεται. ⟩

_____

2 5 λέγει Ἰησοῦς Grenfell-Hunt[1904a] ‖ 6 ζητῶν Grenfell-Hunt[1904a] ‖ τοῦ ζητεῖν Heinrici[1905] ‖ ἕως ἂν . . . (8) βασιλεύσας ἀναπαήσεται Grenfell-Hunt[1904a] ‖ 8 βασιλεύσει : βασιλευση pap.

2 λέγει Ἰησοῦς· μὴ παυσάσθω ὁ ζητῶν τοῦ ζητεῖν ἕως ἂν εὕρῃ, καὶ ὅταν εὕρῃ θαμβηθήσεται, καὶ θαμβηθεὶς βασιλεύσει, καὶ βασιλεύσας ἀναπαήσεται.

Jesus said, 'Let the one who is seeking not stop seeking until he finds. When he finds, he will be amazed. When he is amazed, he will rule. When he rules, he will rest.'

Saying 3

P.Oxy. 654(↓), lines 9–21

```
 9          λέγει Ἰ[η(σοῦ)ς· ἐὰν
10  οἱ ἕλκοντες ὑμᾶς [εἴπωσιν ὑμῖν· ἰδοὺ]
11  ἡ βασιλεία ἐν οὐρα[νῷ, ὑμᾶς φθήσεται]
12  τὰ πετεινὰ τοῦ οὐρ[ανοῦ· ἐὰν δ᾽ εἴπωσιν ὅ-]
13  τι ὑπὸ τὴν γῆν ἐστ[ιν
14  οἱ ἰχθύες τῆς θαλά[σσης
15  τες ὑμᾶς· καὶ ἡ ᾽βασ[ιλεία τοῦ πατρὸς᾽]
16  ἐντὸς ὑμῶν [ἐ]στι [κἀκτός· ὅστις ἂν ἑαυτὸν]
17  γνῷ, ταύτην εὑρή[σει· καὶ ὅτε ὑμεῖς]
18  ἑαυτοὺς γνώσεσθε, [εἴσεσθε ὅτι οἱ υἱοί]
19  ἐστε ᾽ὑμεῖς᾽ τοῦ πατρὸς τοῦ ζ[ῶντος· εἰ δὲ μὴ]
20  γνώσ<εσ>θε ἑαυτούς, ἐν [τῇ πτωχείᾳ ἐστὲ]
21  καὶ ὑμεῖς ἐστε ἡ πτω[χεία. ⤷]
```

3 9 Ἰησοῦς Grenfell-Hunt[1904a] ‖ ἐὰν οἱ . . . (12) εἴπωσιν ὅτι Fitzmyer[1959] ‖ 10 ὑμᾶς : ημας pap. ‖ 13 ὑπὸ : ὑπο pap. ‖ ἐστιν Grenfell-Hunt[1904a] ‖ 14 ἰχθύες : ἰχθυες pap. ‖ θαλάσσης Grenfell-Hunt[1904a] ‖ 15 ὑμᾶς : ὑμας pap. ‖ βασιλεία τοῦ πατρὸς Kasser[1961] : βασιλεία τῶν οὐρανῶν Grenfell-Hunt[1904a] : βασιλεία τοῦ θεοῦ Fitzmyer[1959] ‖ 16 κἀκτός Fitzmyer[1959] ‖ ὅστις ἂν ἑαυτὸν Grenfell-Hunt[1904a] ‖ 17 εὑρήσει Grenfell-Hunt[1904a] ‖ καὶ ὅτε ὑμεῖς Fitzmyer[1959] ‖ 18 γνώσεσθε : γνωσεσθα[ι] pap. ‖ εἴσεσθε Fitzmyer[1959] : εἰδήσετε Grenfell-Hunt[1904a] ‖ ὅτι οἱ υἱοί Bernhard : ὅτι υἱοί Grenfell-Hunt[1904a] ‖ 19 ᾽ὑμεῖς᾽ : ᾽ὑμεις᾽ pap. ‖ ζῶντος· εἰ . . . (21) ἡ πτωχεία Fitzmyer[1959] ‖ 21 ὑμεῖς : ὑμεις pap.

3 λέγει Ἰησοῦς· ἐὰν οἱ ἕλκοντες ὑμᾶς εἴπωσιν ὑμῖν· ἰδοὺ ἡ βασιλεία ἐν οὐρανῷ, ὑμᾶς φθήσεται τὰ πετεινὰ τοῦ οὐρανοῦ· ἐὰν δ εἴπωσιν ὅτι ὑπὸ τὴν γῆν ἐστιν ... οἱ ἰχθύες τῆς θαλάσσης ... ὑμᾶς· καὶ ἡ βασιλεία τοῦ πατρὸς ἐντὸς ὑμῶν ἐστι κἀκτός· ὅστις ἂν ἑαυτὸν γνῷ, ταύτην εὑρήσει· καὶ ὅτε ὑμεῖς ἑαυτοὺς γνώσεσθε, εἴσεσθε ὅτι οἱ υἱοί ἐστε ὑμεῖς τοῦ πατρὸς τοῦ ζῶντος· εἰ δὲ μὴ γνώσεσθε ἑαυτούς, ἐν τῇ πτωχείᾳ ἐστὲ καὶ ὑμεῖς ἐστε ἡ πτωχεία.

Jesus said, 'If those who lead you say to you, "See, the kingdom is in the sky," the birds of the sky will arrive before you. If they say that it is under the earth ... the fish of the sea ... you. The kingdom of the father is in the midst of you and it is outside of you; whoever knows himself will find it. When you know yourselves, you will know that you are the children of the living father. But if you do not know yourselves, you are in poverty and you are poverty.'

Saying 4

P. Oxy. 654(↓), lines 21–27

21   [λέγει Ἰη(σοῦ)ς·]
22 οὐκ ἀποκνήσει ἄνθ[ρωπος παλαιὸς ἡμε-]
23 ρῶν ἐπερωτῆσαι πα[ιδίον τῶν ἑπτὰ ἡμε-]
24 ρῶν περὶ τοῦ τόπου τῆ[ς ζωῆς, καὶ αὐτὸς ζή-]
25 σεται· ˋὅτιˊ πολλοὶ ἔσονται π[ρῶτοι ἔσχατοι καὶ]
26 οἱ ἔσχατοι πρῶτοι, καὶ [εἰς ἓν καταντήσου-]
27 σιν.

_____

4 21 λέγει Ἰησοῦς Grenfell-Hunt¹⁹⁰⁴ᵃ ‖ 22 ἄνθρωπος Grenfell-Hunt¹⁹⁰⁴ᵃ ‖ παλαιὸς ἡμερῶν Hofius¹⁹⁶⁰ : πλήρης ἡμερῶν Taylor¹⁹⁰⁵ ‖ 23 ἐπερωτῆσαι : επερωτησε pap. ‖ παιδίον τῶν ἑπτὰ ἡμερῶν Nations¹⁹⁶⁰ : παιδίον ἑπτὰ ἡμερῶν Fitzmyer¹⁹⁵⁹ ‖ 24 τῆς ζωῆς, καὶ Fitzmyer¹⁹⁵⁹ ‖ [αὐτὸς ζή]σεται Kasser¹⁹⁶¹ : [ζή]σεται Hofius¹⁹⁶⁰ :]σετε pap. ‖ 25 πρῶτοι ἔσχατοι καὶ Grenfell-Hunt¹⁹⁰⁴ᵃ ‖ 26 εἰς ἓν καταντήσουσιν Marcovich¹⁹⁶⁹ : εἰς γενήσουσιν Hofius¹⁹⁶⁰

4 λέγει Ἰησοῦς· οὐκ ἀποκνήσει ἄνθρωπος παλαιὸς ἡμερῶν ἐπερωτῆσαι παιδίον τῶν ἑπτὰ ἡμερῶν περὶ τοῦ τόπου τῆς ζωῆς, καὶ αὐτὸς ζήσεται· ὅτι πολλοὶ ἔσονται πρῶτοι ἔσχατοι καὶ οἱ ἔσχατοι πρῶτοι, καὶ εἰς ἓν καταντήσουσιν.

Jesus said, 'A person old in days will not hesitate to ask a child seven days old about the place of life, and he will live. For many who are first will be last and the last first, and they will become one.'

Saying 5

P.Oxy. 654(↓), lines 27–31

27   λέγει Ἰη(σοῦ)ς· ✕ γ[νῶθι τὸ ὂν ἔμπροσ-]
28 θεν τῆς ὄψεώς σου, καὶ [τὸ κεκαλυμμένον]
29 ἀπό σου ἀποκαλυφ<θ>ήσετ[αί σοι· οὐ γάρ ἐσ-]
30 τιν κρυπτὸν ὃ οὐ φαγε[ρὸν γενήσεται,]
31 καὶ τεθαμμένον ὃ ο[ὐκ ἐγερθήσεται.]

---

5 27 γνῶθι τὸ ὂν Fitzmyer[1959] ‖ ἔμπροσθεν Grenfell-Hunt[1904a] ‖ 28 τὸ κεκαλυμμένον Evelyn-White[1920] : τὸ κεκρυμμένον Grenfell-Hunt[1904a] ‖ 29 ἀποκαλυφθήσεταί σοι … (31) οὐκ ἐγερθήσεται Grenfell-Hunt[1904a] ‖ 31 τεθαμμένον : θεθαμμενον pap.

5 λέγει Ἰησοῦς· γνῶθι τὸ ὂν ἔμπροσθεν τῆς ὄψεώς σου, καὶ τὸ κεκαλυμμένον ἀπό σου ἀποκαλυφθήσεταί σοι· οὐ γάρ ἐστιν κρυπτὸν ὃ οὐ φανερὸν γενήσεται, καὶ τεθαμμένον ὃ οὐκ ἐγερθήσεται.

Jesus said, 'Know what is in front of your face, and what is hidden from you will be revealed to you. For there is nothing hidden that will not be disclosed and nothing buried that will not be raised.'

Saying 6+7

P.Oxy. 654(↓), lines 32–42

32 [ἐξ]ετάζουσιν αὐτὸν ο[ἱ μαθηταὶ αὐτοῦ καὶ]
33 [λέ]γουσιν· πῶς νηστεύ[σομεν; καὶ πῶς προσ-]
34 [ευξό]μεθα; καὶ πῶς [ἐλεημοσύνην ποιήσο-]
35 [μεν; κ]αὶ τί παρατηρήσ[ομεν περὶ τῶν βρω-]
36 [μάτω]ν; ✕ λέγει Ἰη(σοῦ)ς· [μὴ ψεύδεσθε καὶ ὅ-]
37 [τι μισ]εῖτε μὴ ποιεῖτ[ε
38   τ]ῆς ἀληθ[ε]ίας αν[. . . . . οὐδὲν]
39 [γάρ ἐστι]ν ἀ[π]οκεκρ[υμμένον ὃ οὐ φανερὸν]
40 [ἔσται. μα]κάρι[ός] ἐστιν [ὁ λέων ὃν φάγεται]
41 [ἄνθρωπος καὶ ὁ λέ]ων ἔστ[αι ἄνθρωπος· καὶ]
42 [οὐαὶ τῷ ἀνθρώπῳ] ὃν [φάγεται λέων

6+7 32 ἐξετάζουσιν αὐτὸν . . . (33) καὶ πῶς Grenfell-Hunt[1904a] ‖ 33 προσευξόμεθα Bruston[1905] : προσευξώμεθα Swete[1904] ‖ 34 ἐλεημοσύνην ποιήσομεν Evelyn-White[1920] : ἐλεημοσύνην ποιήσωμεν Swete[1904] ‖ 35 παρατηρήσομεν Grenfell-Hunt[1904a] ‖ περὶ τῶν βρωμάτων Hofius[1960] ‖ 36 μὴ ψεύδεσθε καὶ ὅτι μισεῖτε Fitzmyer[1959] ‖ 37 [μισ]εῖτε : [μισ]ειται pap. ‖ 38 οὐδὲν γάρ . . . (39) φανερὸν ἔσται Fitzmyer[1959] ‖ 40 μακάριός Grenfell-Hunt[1904a] ‖ ὁ λέων ὃν φάγεται ἄνθρωπος καὶ Kasser[1961] ‖ 41 ὁ λέων Marcovich[1969] : λέων Kasser[1961] ‖ ἔσται ἄνθρωπος· καὶ Kasser[1961] ‖ 42 οὐαὶ τῷ ἀνθρώπῳ Lührmann[1990] : ἀνάθεμα ὁ ἄνθρωπος Attridge[1989] ‖ φάγεται λέων Lührmann[1990]

6+7 ἐξετάζουσιν αὐτὸν οἱ μαθηταὶ αὐτοῦ καὶ λέγουσιν· πῶς νηστεύσομεν; καὶ πῶς προσευξόμεθα; καὶ πῶς ἐλεημοσύνην ποιήσομεν; καὶ τί παρατηρήσομεν περὶ τῶν βρωμάτων; λέγει Ἰησοῦς· μὴ ψεύδεσθε καὶ ὅτι μισεῖτε μὴ ποιεῖτε ... τῆς ἀληθείας ... οὐδὲν γάρ ἐστιν ἀποκεκρυμμένον ὃ οὐ φανερὸν ἔσται. μακάριός ἐστιν ὁ λέων ὃν φάγεται ἄνθρωπος καὶ ὁ λέων ἔσται ἄνθρωπος· καὶ οὐαὶ τῷ ἀνθρώπῳ ὃν φάγεται λέων ...

His disciples questioned him and said, 'How are we to fast? How are we to pray? How are we to perform charitable deeds? What diet are we to observe?'

Jesus said, 'Do not lie and do not do what you hate ... of the truth ... For there is nothing hidden that will not be disclosed. Blessed is the lion that a human being will eat, for the lion will become human. And how unfortunate is the human being that a lion will eat ...'

Saying 24(?)

P.Oxy. 655, fragment d

1   ἐσ]τιν
2   φ]ωτ῾ε῾ινῷ
3   κ]όσμῳ
4   ]η
5   ἐ]στιν.

Saying 26

P.Oxy. 1(↓), lines 1–4

1 καὶ τότε διαβλέψεις
2 ἐκβαλεῖν τὸ κάρφος
3 τὸ ἐν τῷ ὀφθαλμῷ 7
4 τοῦ ἀδελφοῦ σου.

... is
... full of light
... world
. . .
... is

26 ... καὶ τότε διαβλέψεις ἐκβαλεῖν τὸ κάρφος τὸ ἐν τῷ ὀφθαλμῷ τοῦ ἀδελφοῦ σου.

'... and then you will see clearly to take out the speck that is in your brother's eye.'

Saying 27

P.Oxy. 1(↓), lines 4–11

```
 4                    λέγει
 5  Ἰ(ησοῦ)ς· ἐὰν μὴ νηστεύση-
 6  τε τὸν κόσμον, οὐ μὴ
 7  εὕρητε τὴν βασιλεί-
 8  αν τοῦ θ(εο)ῦ· καὶ ἐὰν μὴ
 9  σαββατίσητε τὸ σάβ- ⌐
10  βατον, οὐκ ὄψεσθε τὸ(ν)
11  π(ατέ)ρα.
```

27 5 νηστεύσητε : νηστευσηται pap. ‖ 7 εὕρητε : ευρηται pap.

27 λέγει Ἰησοῦς· ἐὰν μὴ νηστεύσητε τὸν κόσμον, οὐ μὴ εὕρητε τὴν βασιλείαν τοῦ θεοῦ· καὶ ἐὰν μὴ σαββατίσητε τὸ σάββατον, οὐκ ὄψεσθε τὸν πατέρα.

Jesus said, 'If you do not fast with respect to the world, you will not find the kingdom of God. And if you do not keep the Sabbath a Sabbath, you will not see the father.'

Saying 28

P. Oxy. 1(↓), lines 11–22

11   λέγει Ἰ(ησοῦ)ς· ἔ[σ]την
12   ἐν μέσῳ τοῦ κόσμου
13   καὶ ἐν σαρκὶ ὤφθην
14   αὐτοῖς καὶ εὗρον πάν-
15   τας μεθύοντας καὶ
16   οὐδένα εὗρον διψῶ(ν)-
17   τα ἐν αὐτοῖς· καὶ πο- ⏋
18   νεῖ ἡ ψυχή μου ἐπὶ ⏋
19   τοῖς υἱοῖς τῶν ἀν(θρώπ)ων
20   ὅτι τυφλοί εἰσιν τῇ καρ-
21   δίᾳ αὐτῶ[ν] κ̣α̣ὶ̣ [οὐ] βλέπ-
22   [ουσιν.

Saying 29

P. Oxy. 1(→), lines 0–1

0   ἐνοι-]
1   [κ]ε̣ῖ [ταύτ]η̣[ν τ]ὴν πτωχˋεˊία(ν).

---

28 13 σαρκὶ : σαρκει (with ε deleted by ancient scribe) pap. ‖ 16 διψῶ(ν)τα : δειψωτα pap. ‖
19 υἱοῖς : ϋιοις pap. ‖ 21 αὐτῶν καὶ οὐ βλέπουσιν Grenfell-Hunt[1898]
29 0 ἐνοικεῖ ταύτην τὴν Fitzmyer[1959]

28 λέγει Ἰησοῦς· ἔστην ἐν μέσῳ τοῦ κόσμου καὶ ἐν σαρκὶ ὤφθην αὐτοῖς καὶ εὗρον πάντας μεθύοντας καὶ οὐδένα εὗρον διψῶντα ἐν αὐτοῖς· καὶ πονεῖ ἡ ψυχή μου ἐπὶ τοῖς υἱοῖς τῶν ἀνθρώπων ὅτι τυφλοί εἰσιν τῇ καρδίᾳ αὐτῶν καὶ οὐ βλέπουσιν.

Jesus said, 'I stood in the midst of the world and I appeared to them in the flesh. I found that all were drunk; indeed, I found that not one among them was thirsty. My soul is troubled on account of the children of humanity because they are blind in their hearts and do not see.'

29 . . . ἐνοικεῖ ταύτην τὴν πτωχείαν.

'. . . dwells in this poverty.'

Saying 30+77b

P.Oxy. 1(→), lines 2–9

2 [λέγ]ει ['Ι(ησοῦ)ς· ὅπ]ου ἐὰν ὦσιν
3 ['τρ]ε[ῖς], ε[ἰσὶ]ν ἄθεοι·' καὶ
4 [ὅ]που ε[ἷς] ἐστιν μόνος,
5 [λέ]γω, ἐγώ εἰμι μετ' αὐ-
6 τ[οῦ.] ἔγει[ρ]ον τὸν λίθο(ν)
7 κἀκεῖ εὑρήσεις με·
8 σχίσον τὸ ξύλον κἀγὼ
9 ἐκεῖ εἰμι.

Saying 31

P.Oxy. 1(→), lines 9–14

9   λέγει 'Ι(ησοῦ)ς· οὐ-
10 κ ἔστιν δεκτὸς προ-
11 φήτης ἐν τῇ π(ατ)ρίδι αὐ-
12 τ[ο]ῦ, οὐδὲ ἰατρὸς ποιεῖ
13 θεραπείας εἰς τοὺς
14 γινώσκοντας αὐτό(ν).

30+77b 2 λέγει 'Ιησοῦς· ὅπου Grenfell-Hunt[1897] ‖ 3 τρεῖς, εἰσὶν ἄθεοι Attridge[1979] : τρεῖς, εἰσὶν θεοί Akagi[1965] : γ' θεοί, εἰσὶν θεοί Guillaumont[1958] : δύο (or β'), οὐκ εἰσὶν ἄθεοι Blass[1897] ‖ 4 ὅπου εἷς Blass[1897] ‖ 5 λέγω Grenfell-Hunt[1898] ‖ αὐτοῦ. ἔγειρον Grenfell-Hunt[1897]
31 14 γινώσκοντας : γεινωσκοντας pap.

30+77b λέγει Ἰησοῦς· ὅπου ἐὰν ὦσιν τρεῖς, εἰσὶν ἄθεοι· καὶ ὅπου εἷς ἐστιν μόνος, λέγω, ἐγώ εἰμι μετ᾽ αὐτοῦ. ἔγειρον τὸν λίθον κἀκεῖ εὑρήσεις με· σχίσον τὸ ξύλον κἀγὼ ἐκεῖ εἰμι.

Jesus said, 'Where there are three, they are without God. Where there is one alone, I say, I am with him. Lift up the stone and you will find me there. Split the wood and I am there.'

31 λέγει Ἰησοῦς· οὐκ ἔστιν δεκτὸς προφήτης ἐν τῇ πατρίδι αὐτοῦ, οὐδὲ ἰατρὸς ποιεῖ θεραπείας εἰς τοὺς γινώσκοντας αὐτόν.

Jesus said, 'A prophet is not accepted in his homeland; nor does a physician perform healings for those who know him.'

Saying 32

P. Oxy. 1 (→), lines 15–20

15 λέγει Ἰ(ησοῦ)ς· πόλις ῳκοδο-
16 μημένη ἐπ᾽ ἄκρον
17 [ὄ]ρους ὑψηλοῦ καὶ ἐσ-
18 τηριγμένη οὔτε πε-
19 [σ]εῖν δύναται οὔτε κρυ-
20 [β]ῆναι.

Saying 33

P. Oxy. 1 (→), lines 20–21

20   λέγει Ἰ(ησοῦ)ς· <ὃ> ἀκούεις
21 [ε]ἰς τὸ ἓν ὠτίον σου, τὸ[

---

32 15 ῳκοδομημένη : οικοδομημενη pap. ‖ 17 ὑψηλοῦ : υψηλους pap.

32 λέγει Ἰησοῦς· πόλις ᾠκοδομημένη ἐπ' ἄκρον ὄρους ὑψηλοῦ καὶ ἐστηριγμένη οὔτε πεσεῖν δύναται οὔτε κρυβῆναι.

Jesus said, 'A city built on top of a high mountain and fortified can neither fall nor be hidden.'

33 λέγει Ἰησοῦς· ὃ ἀκούεις εἰς τὸ ἓν ὠτίον σου . . .

Jesus said, 'What you hear in your one ear . . .'

Saying 36

P.Oxy. 655, column i, lines 0–17

0   [λέγει Ἰ(ησοῦ)ς· μὴ μεριμνᾶ-]
1   [τε ἀ]πὸ πρωῒ ἕ[ως ὀψέ,]
2   [μήτ]ε ἀφ᾽ ἑσπ[έρας]
3   [ἕως π]ρωῒ, μήτε [τῇ]
4   [τροφῇ ὑ]μῶν τί φά-
5   [γητε, μήτε] τῇ στ[ο-]
6   [λῇ ὑμῶν] τί ἐνδύ-
7   [ση]σθε. [πολ]λῷ κρεί[σ-]
8   [σον]ές ἐ[στε] τῶν [κρί-]
9   νων, ῾ἅτι[να ο]ὐ ξα[ί-]
10   νει οὐδὲ ν[ήθ]ει μ[ηδ-]
11   ἐν ἔχοντ[α ἔ]νδ[υ-]
12   μα. τί ἐν[δύεσθε] καὶ
13   ὑμεῖς;᾽ τίς ἂν προσθ<εί>η
14   ἐπὶ τὴν ἡλικίαν
15   ὑμῶν; αὐτὸ[ς δ]ώσει
16   ὑμῖν τὸ ἔνδυμα ὑ-
17   μῶν.

36 0 λέγει Ἰησοῦς· μὴ μεριμνᾶτε Fitzmyer[1959] ‖ 1 ἀπὸ πρωὶ . . . (8) τῶν κρίνων Grenfell-Hunt[1904a] ‖ 9 ἅτι[να ο]ὐ ξα[ί]νει οὐδὲ ν[ήθ]ει μ[ηδ]ὲν ἔχοντ[α ἔ]νδ[υ]μα. τί ἐν[δύεσθε] καὶ ὑμεῖς; Bernhard : ἅτι[να ο]ὐ ξα[ί]νει οὐδὲ ν[ήθ]ει. μ[ηδ]ὲν ἔχοντ[ες ἔ]νδ[υ]μα, τί ἐν[δύεσθε] καὶ ὑμεῖς; Attridge[1989] : ἅτι[να ο]ὐ ξα[ί]νει οὐδὲ ν[ήθ]ει μ[ηδ]ὲν ἔχοντ[α ἔ]νδ[υ]μα. τί ἐν[δεῖτε] καὶ ὑμεῖς; Lührmann[2000] : ἅτι[να α]ὐξάνει οὐδὲ ν[ήθ]ει μ[ηδ]ὲν ἔχοντ[α ἔ]νδ[υ]μα. τί ἐνδεῖτε] καὶ ὑμεῖς; Fitzmyer[1959] ‖ οὐ ξαίνει Bartlet[1905] : αὐξάνει Grenfell-Hunt[1904a] ‖ 11 ἔχοντα Zahn[1905] : ἔχοντες Grenfell-Hunt[1904a] ‖ 12 ἐνδύεσθε Hilgenfeld[1904] : ἐνδεῖτε Grenfell-Hunt[1904c] ‖ 14 ἡλικίαν : ειλικιαν pap. ‖ 15 αὐτὸς δώσει Grenfell-Hunt[1904a] ‖ 16 ὑμῖν : υμειν pap.

36 λέγει Ἰησοῦς· μὴ μεριμνᾶτε ἀπὸ πρωῒ ἕως ὀψέ, μήτε ἀφ᾽ ἑσπέρας ἕως πρωῒ, μήτε τῇ τροφῇ ὑμῶν τί φάγητε, μήτε τῇ στολῇ ὑμῶν τί ἐνδύσησθε. πολλῷ κρείσσονές ἐστε τῶν κρίνων, ἅτινα οὐ ξαίνει οὐδὲ νήθει μηδὲν ἔχοντα ἔνδυμα. τί ἐνδύεσθε καὶ ὑμεῖς; τίς ἂν προσθείη ἐπὶ τὴν ἡλικίαν ὑμῶν; αὐτὸς δώσει ὑμῖν τὸ ἔνδυμα ὑμῶν.

Jesus said, 'Do not be anxious from morning until evening or from evening until morning, either about what you will eat as your food or about what you will wear as your robe. You are much better than the lilies, which neither card nor spin, even though they have no clothing. And you, what do you wear? Who can add to your lifespan? He is the one who will give your clothing to you.'

Saying 37

P. Oxy. 655, column i, line 17 – column ii, line 1

17   λέγουσιν αὐ-
18 τῷ οἱ μαθηταὶ αὐτοῦ·
19 πότε ἡμῖν ἐμφα-
20 νὴς ἔσει, καὶ πότε
21 σε ὀψόμεθα; λέγει·
22 ὅταν ἐκδύσησθε καὶ
23 μὴ αἰσχυνθῆτε. [
   [approximately 7 lines lost]
 1 θ[

Saying 38(?)

P. Oxy. 655, column ii, lines 2–11

 2 λέ[γει Ἰ(ησοῦ)ς
 3 ο[
 4 τα̣[
 5 γυ̣[
 6 κα̣[
 7 νρ[
 8 κα[
 9 ημ̣[
10 σε̣[
11 [

37 λέγουσιν αὐτῷ οἱ μαθηταὶ αὐτοῦ· πότε ἡμῖν ἐμφανὴς ἔσει, καὶ πότε σε ὀψόμεθα; λέγει· ὅταν ἐκδύσησθε καὶ μὴ αἰσχυνθῆτε . . .

His disciples said to him, 'When will you be revealed to us? And when will we see you?'
He said, 'When you strip and are not ashamed . . .'

Jesus said . . .
. . .
. . .
. . .
. . .
. . .
. . .
. . .
. . .
. . .

Saying 39

P.Oxy. 655, column ii, lines 12–23

12 [λέγει Ἰ(ησοῦ)ς· οἱ Φαρισαῖοι]
13 [καὶ οἱ γραμματεῖς]
14 ἔλ[αβον τὰς κλεῖδας]
15 τῆς [γνώσεως καὶ ἔ-]
16 κρυψ[αν αὐτάς· οὔτε]
17 εἰσῆλ[θον οὔτε τοὺς]
18 εἰσερ[χομένους ἀφῆ-]
19 καν [εἰσελθεῖν. ὑμεῖς]
20 δὲ γί[νεσθε φρόνι-]
21 μοι ὡ[ς οἱ ὄφεις καὶ ἀ-]
22 κέραι[οι ὡς αἱ περιστε-]
23 ρα[ί.

---

39 12 λέγει Ἰησοῦς ... (13) οἱ γραμματεῖς Fitzmyer[1959] ‖ 14 ἔλαβον Michelsen[1905] ‖ τὰς κλεῖδας Allen[1904] : τὴν κλεῖδα Grenfell-Hunt[1904a] ‖ 15 γνώσεως Grenfell-Hunt[1904a] ‖ καὶ Fitzmyer[1959] ‖ ἔκρυψαν Allen[1904] ‖ 16 αὐτάς. οὔτε Fitzmyer[1959] ‖ 17 εἰσῆλθον οὔτε τοὺς Kraft[1961] : εἰσῆλθον οὐδὲ τοὺς Allen[1904] ‖ 18 εἰσερχομένους ἀφῆκαν ... (22) αἱ περιστεραί Allen[1904] ‖ 20 γί[νεσθε] : γει[νεσθε] pap.

39 λέγει Ἰησοῦς· οἱ Φαρισαῖοι καὶ οἱ γραμματεῖς ἔλαβον τὰς κλεῖδας τῆς γνώσεως καὶ ἔκρυψαν αὐτάς· οὔτε εἰσῆλθον οὔτε τοὺς εἰσερχομένους ἀφῆκαν εἰσελθεῖν. ὑμεῖς δὲ γίνεσθε φρόνιμοι ὡς οἱ ὄφεις καὶ ἀκέραιοι ὡς αἱ περιστεραί.

Jesus said, 'The Pharisees and the scribes have taken the keys of knowledge and hidden them. They have not entered, nor have they allowed those who were trying to enter to do so. You, however, be wise as snakes and innocent as doves.'

Unidentifiable fragments of Oxyrhynchus Papyrus 655

P. Oxy. 655, fragment e

1 . . .
2 κο[

P. Oxy. 655, fragment f

1 . . .
2]κα[
3 . . .

P. Oxy. 655, fragment g

1 . . .
2]κ . [
3]αι[
4 . . .

P. Oxy. 655, fragment h

1 . . .
2]ε[
3 . . .

THE GOSPEL OF PETER

During the winter of 1886–87, a French archaeological team discovered a small parchment codex at a cemetery in Akhmim, Egypt.[1] Careful examination of the codex revealed that it contained a nine-page excerpt of a gospel written in the first person from the perspective of Jesus' most famous disciple, Peter. The first modern edition of this 'Akhmim Fragment' of the *Gospel of Peter* (P.Cair. 10759) was published in 1892 and inspired a brief frenzy of scholarly activity.[2] Before the end of the decade, a host of editions, translations and commentaries had been released.

Since the end of the nineteenth century, two additional fragments of the text have been recognized among the Oxyrhynchus papyri. These small fragments, which were originally published in 1972 and 1994, can both be dated to the second century. The first, P.Oxy. 2949, was identified because it preserves a label for Joseph of Arimathea ('the friend of Pilate') known only from P.Cair. 10759 (*Gos. Pet.* 2.3). The second, P.Oxy. 4009, uses the first person to narrate a discussion between Jesus and Peter that is also recounted in the ancient Christian homily known as *2 Clement* (5.2–4).

The *Gospel of Peter* was a narrative gospel similar to Matthew, Mark, Luke and John. The full contents of the gospel are not known. The dialogue between Peter and Jesus preserved on P.Oxy. 4009 was probably placed in the context of Jesus' ministry. P.Cair. 10759 contains an extended

---

1. Akhmim (ancient Panopolis) is a city located roughly 250 miles south of Cairo. It has often been reported that the codex was recovered from the tomb of a medieval monk but this is not completely certain. See P. van Minnen, 'The Greek Apocalypse of Peter', in *The Apocalypse of Peter* (eds. J. N. Bremmer and I. Czachesz; Studies on Early Christian Apocrypha, 7; Leuven: Peeters, 2003), pp. 17–18. "The first editor of the Akhmim codex claims that it was found in the tomb of a monk. This was no doubt merely an inference from the content of the codex, not based on actual indications in the tomb itself. The inference may be correct, but it should not be used as an independent fact in discussing the codex." See also the similiar comments in T. J. Kraus and T. Nicklas, *Das Petrusevangelium und die Petrusapokalypse: Die griechischen Fragmente mit deutscher und englischer Übersetzung* (Berlin: Walter de Gruyter, 2004), pp. 25–27.

2. Eusebius reports that a dispute over a *Gospel of Peter* erupted in the Christian commuity at Rhossus near the end of the second century CE (*Hist. eccl.* 6.12). It can only be assumed that the gospel excerpt in the codex found at Akhmim is a part of the same text; no title for the text is actually given in the codex.

passion narrative that begins abruptly with the trial of Jesus before Pilate and breaks off mid-sentence at what appears to be the beginning of an otherwise unknown resurrection appearance. P.Oxy. 2949 overlaps with part of P.Cair. 10759. The contents of the resurrection appearance and anything else that may have been included in the gospel have been completely lost.

The modern textual divisions used with the *Gospel of Peter* are somewhat unusual. On the basis of P.Cair. 10759, the gospel was originally divided into 14 chapters and 60 verses by scholars working independently, and later editors combined the two systems of notation. As a result, both chapter and verse numbers increase continuously throughout the text (e.g., *Gos. Pet.* 3.6 is the opening verse of chapter 3). P.Oxy. 2949 is usually associated with *Gos. Pet.* 2.3–5, although it was apparently not identical to the version of the text preserved on P.Cair. 10759. P.Oxy. 4009 has to be left without chapter and verse numbers because it likely preceded the passage that has been treated as *Gos. Pet.* 1.1.

*   *   *   *

Two other Greek manuscripts that might be considered in association with the *Gospel of Peter* are P.Vindob.G 2325 and P.Oxy. 1224. P.Vindob.G 2325 would have to be identified as a part of the *Gospel of Peter*, if the restoration of the first person pronoun immediately before Peter's name in line 5 were certain.[3] P.Oxy. 1224 would have to be identified as a part of the *Gospel of Peter*, if it could be shown that Peter were the purported narrator of this apparently first-person gospel.[4] However, the restoration of the first person pronoun in line 5 of P.Vindob.G 2325 is hypothetical (i.e., uncertain and unnecessary) and the identity of the narrator of the gospel preserved on P.Oxy. 1224 remains uncertain. Thus, it has seemed best to include P.Vindob.G 2325 and P.Oxy. 1224 with the other unidentified gospel fragments in this book.

---

3. See D. Lührmann, 'POx 4009: Ein neues Fragment des Petrusevangeliums?', *NovT* 35 (1993), pp. 390–410 (407); D. Lührmann and E. Schlarb, *Fragmente apokryph gewordener Evangelien in griechischer und lateinischer Sprache* (Marburger theologische Studien, 59; Marburg, Germany: N.G. Elwert Verlag, 2000), p. 74. In *Fragmente apokryph gewordener Evangelien*, Lührmann treats P.Vindob.G 2325 as a part of the *Gospel of Peter* but notes that his identification of the papyrus fragment is still only a hypothesis: 'Sollte diese Vermutung nicht stimmen, bleibt P.Vindob. G 2325 ein unidentifiziertes Fragment; versuchsweise sei es dem EvPetr zugeordnet.'

4. V. Bartlet first suggested that P.Oxy. 1224 preserved a small part of the *Gospel of Peter*. His suggestion is reported in B. P. Grenfell and A. S. Hunt, '1224. Uncanonical Gospel', in vol. 10 of *The Oxyrhynchus Papyri* (London: Egypt Exploration Fund, 1914), pp. 1–10 (4).

Oxyrhynchus Papyrus 4009 (P.Oxy. 4009)

Contents: A first-person account of a discussion between Peter (?) and Jesus (cf. *2 Clem.* 5.2–4; Lk. 10.2–3; Mt. 9.37–38; 10.16), evidently a part of the *Gospel of Peter* that preceded what has been labelled *Gos. Pet.* 1.1.

Date copied: Second century (Lührmann and Parsons).

Basic description: Papyrus codex; part of one leaf, w. 2.9 x h. 9.0 cm; 41 partially preserved lines of text.

Nomina sacra: κε̄ (κύριε).

Other notable features: Punctuation in the form of the middle point and as small blank space at the ends of sentences; paragraphing apparently by blank line-end in (→).10 and by ecthesis in (↓).10; some final nus suppressed, indicated by a supralinear stroke over the preceding letter.

Current housing location: Sackler Library, University of Oxford.

Museum ID: P.Oxy.LX 4009.

First published edition: D. Lührmann, 'POx 4009: Ein neues Fragment des Petrusevangeliums?', *NovT* 35 (1993), pp. 390–410.

Official publication: D. Lührmann and P. J. Parsons, '4009.Gospel of Peter?', in vol. 60 of *The Oxyrhynchus Papyri* (eds. R. A. Coles, M. W. Haslam and P. J. Parsons; London: Egypt Exploration Society, 1994), pp. 1–5.

The Akhmim Fragment (P.Cair. 10759)

Contents: Gos. Pet. 1.1–14.60 (see 'Basic description' for information about non-gospel texts found in the codex).

Date copied: Late sixth century (Cavallo and Maehler).

Basic description: Parchment (vellum) codex; thirty-three well-preserved leaves, average w. 13.0 x h. 16.0 cm; 154 mostly preserved lines of gospel text on pages 2–10; page 1 is a decorated cover; pages 11–12 are blank; pages 13–19 contain a fragment of the *Apocalypse of Peter* (bound upside down); page 20 is blank; pages 21–66 contain a portion of the *Book of Enoch*; a vellum leaf from another manuscript inserted into the binding contains part of the *Acts of St. Julian.*

Nomina sacra: ᾱνο̄ς (ἄνθρωπος); ᾱνω̄ν (ἀνθρώπων); θ̄υ (θεοῦ); κ̄ς (κύριος); κ̄υ (κυρίου); κ̄ν (κύριον).

Other notable features: Crosses drawn on the manuscript in various places along with a 'coil' beneath the last line of gospel text; some final nus suppressed, indicated by a supralinear stroke over the preceding letter.

Current housing location: Egyptian Museum, Cairo.

First published edition: U. Bouriant, *Fragments du texte grec du livre d'Enoch et de quelques écrits attribués à saint Pierre* (MMAF, 9.1; Paris: Ernest Leroux, 1892).

Correction of first published edition + colour manuscript photos: A. Lods,

Reproduction en héliogravure du manuscrit d'Enoch et des écrits attribués à saint Pierre (MMAF, 9.3; Paris: Ernest Leroux, 1893).

First published edition with chapters: J. A. T. Robinson and M. R. James, *The Gospel According to Peter, and the Revelation of Peter: Two Lectures on the Newly Recovered Fragments Together with the Greek Texts* (London: C. J. Clay and Sons, 1892).

First published edition with verses: A. Harnack, *Bruchstücke des Evangeliums und der Apokalypse des Petrus* (Leipzig: J. C. Hinrichs'sche Buchhandlung, 1893).

Critical edition: T. J. Kraus and T. Nicklas, *Das Petrusevangelium und die Petrusapokalypse: Die griechischen Fragmente mit deutscher und englischer Übersetzung* (Berlin: Walter de Gruyter, 2004).

Other important published edition + colour manuscript photos: O. von Gebhardt, *Das Evangelium und die Apokalypse des Petrus* (Leipzig: J. C. Hinrichs'sche Buchhandlung, 1893).

Oxyrhynchus Papyrus 2949 (P.Oxy. 2949)

Contents: Gos. Pet. 2.3–5 (apparently a somewhat different version than the one preserved on P.Cair. 10759).

Date copied: Late second or early third century (Coles).

Basic Description: Papyrus roll(?); two fragments, w. 4.0 x h. 7.5 cm (fragment 1), w. 1.7 x h. 2.6 cm (fragment 2); 15 partially preserved lines of text + space for 2 more that have been completely abraded.

Nomina sacra: None visible.

Current housing location: Sackler Library, University of Oxford.

Museum ID: P.Oxy.XLI 2949.

First published edition (official publication): R. A. Coles, '2949. Fragments of an Apocryphal Gospel(?)', in vol. 41 of *The Oxyrhynchus Papyri* (eds. G. M. Browne, R. A. Coles, J. R. Rea, J. C. Shelton and E. G. Turner; London: Egypt Exploration Society, 1972), pp. 15–16.

Oxyrhynchus Papyrus 4009

P.Oxy. 4009(→)		P.Oxy. 4009(↓)
] . [		] . [
]αεισ[		]ψει[
] . κα[. .]φ		] . υσ . [
] θερισμός		οὐδὲ τῷ[
5 [γίνου δὲ ἀκέ]ραιος ὡς αἱ [πε-]	5	παρεσχ[
[ριστεραὶ κ]αὶ φρόνιμ[ος]		θοντιμ[
[ὡς οἱ ὄφεις.] ἔσεσθε ὡς		κασδια[
[ἀρνία ἀνὰ μέ]σον λύκων.		ὅτι ἀφˋεʹι . [
[εἶπον πρὸς αὐ]τόν· ἐὰν οὖ(ν)		λαιαμα[
10 [σπαραχθῶ]μεν;	10	αὐτῷ εκ[
[ὁ δὲ ἀποκριθεὶς] λέγει μοι· οἱ		μενων[
[λύκοι σπαρά]ξαντες τὸ		νοματ . [
[ἀρνίον οὐ]κέτι αὐτῷ οὐ-		ἀφεῖς κ(ύρι)ε [
[δὲν δύνανται] ποιῆσαι. δι-		] . ουθ . [
15 [ὸ ἐγὼ λέγω ὑ]μῖν· [μὴ] φο-	15	] . μαι[
[βεῖσθε ἀπὸ τῶ]ν ἀπ[οκτε(ν)-]		]προ[
[όντων ὑμᾶ]ς καὶ [μετὰ τὸ]		]πη . [
[ἀποκτεῖναι] μηκέ[τι ποι-]		] . ιν . . [
[ῆσαι δυναμέ]γων [μηδέ(ν).]		] . σραι[
20] ἔχων [	20	] . . . . [
]μει[		

(→) 5 γίνου δὲ . . . (19) δυναμένων μηδέν Lührmann[1993] ‖ 15 [ὑ]μῖν : [υ]μειν pap.
(↓) 8 ἀφˋεʹι . : αφˋεʹι . (with unidentifiable final letter deleted by ancient scribe) pap.

... θερισμός ... γίνου δὲ ἀκέραιος ὡς αἱ περιστεραὶ καὶ φρόνιμος ὡς οἱ ὄφεις. ἔσεσθε ὡς ἀρνία ἀνὰ μέσον λύκων. εἶπον πρὸς αὐτόν· ἐὰν οὖν σπαραχθῶμεν; ὁ δὲ ἀποκριθεὶς λέγει μοι· οἱ λύκοι σπαράξαντες τὸ ἀρνίον οὐκέτι αὐτῷ οὐδὲν δύνανται ποιῆσαι. διὸ ἐγὼ λέγω ὑμῖν· μὴ φοβεῖσθε ἀπὸ τῶν ἀποκτενόντων ὑμᾶς καὶ μετὰ τὸ ἀποκτεῖναι μηκέτι ποιῆσαι δυναμένων μηδέν ...

'... harvest ... But be innocent as doves and wise as snakes. You will be as sheep in the midst of wolves.'

I† said to him, 'So what if we get torn apart?'

He answered me, 'Wolves tear a sheep apart but can do nothing more to it. Therefore, I say to you, "Do not be afraid of those who kill you but can do nothing more after they kill ..."'

---

† It can be assumed that the narrator here is Peter. *2 Clem.* 5.2–4 recounts the same exchange in the third person, identifying Peter as the person speaking with Jesus.

Chapter 1

P. Cair. 10759, page 2, lines 1–5

1 τ[ῶν] δὲ Ἰουδαίων οὐδεὶς ἐνίψατο τὰς χεῖρας, οὐδὲ
Ἡρῴδης οὐδέ τις τῶν κριτῶν αὐτοῦ. κạὶ μὴ βουληθέντω(ν)
νίψασθαι ἀνέστη Πειλᾶτος· *2* καὶ τότε κελεύει Ἡρῴδης
ὁ βασιλεὺς ῾παρ[αλη]μφθῆναι᾿ τὸν κ(ύριο)ν, εἰπὼν αὐτοῖς ὅτι
ὅσα ἐκέλευσα ὑμῖν ποιῆσαι αὐτῷ ποιήσατε.

Chapter 2

P. Cair. 10759, page 2, lines 5–14

3 <ε>ἱστήκει δὲ
ἐκεῖ Ἰωσήφ, ὁ φίλος Πειλάτου καὶ τοῦ κ(υρίο)υ, καὶ εἰδὼς ὅτι
σταυρίσκειν αὐτὸν μέλλουσιν ἦλθεν πρὸς τὸν Πειλᾶτον
καὶ ᾔτησε τὸ σῶμα τοῦ κ(υρίο)υ πρὸς ταφήν. *4* καὶ ὁ Πειλᾶτος πέμψας πρὸς Ἡρῴδην ᾔτησεν αὐτοῦ τὸ σῶμα. *5* καὶ ὁ Ἡρῴδης
ἔφη· ἀδελφὲ Πειλᾶτε, εἰ καὶ μή τις αὐτὸν ᾐτήκει, ἡμεῖς
αὐτὸν ἐθάπτομεν, ἐπεὶ καὶ σάββατον ἐπιφώσκει. γέγραπται γὰρ ἐν τῷ νόμῳ ἥλιον μὴ δῦναι ἐπὶ πεφονευμένῳ.
καὶ παρέδωκεν αὐτὸν τῷ λαῷ πρὸ μιᾶς τῶν ἀζύμων,
τῆς ἑορτῆς αὐτῶν.

---

1 1 Πειλᾶτος : πειλατης ms. ‖ 2 παραλημφθῆναι Bouriant[1892] : παραπεμφθῆναι Manchot[1893]
‖ ὑμῖν : ϋμιν ms.
2 3 Ἰωσήφ : ϊωσηφ ms.

1 ... but none of the Jews washed his hands, nor did Herod or any of his judges. And since they were not willing to wash, Pilate stood up. *2* Then Herod the king ordered that the Lord be taken away, saying to them, 'Do everything that I ordered you to do to him.'

3 Now Joseph, the friend of Pilate and of the Lord, had been standing there. When he realized that they were about to crucify him, he came to Pilate and asked for the Lord's body for burial. *4* So Pilate sent to Herod and asked for his body.

5 Herod said, 'Brother Pilate, even if nobody had asked for him, we would have buried him because the Sabbath is coming on. For it is written in the law that the sun must not set on one who has been put to death.' And he delivered him to the people before the first day of their Feast of Unleavened Bread.

Chapter 3

P. Cair. 10759, page 2, lines 14–19; page 3, lines 1–4

6 οἱ δὲ λαβόντες τὸν κ(ύριο)ν ὤθουν αὐτὸν
τρέχοντες καὶ ἔλεγον· σύρωμεν τὸν υἱὸν τοῦ θ(εο)ῦ ἐξουσίαν
αὐτοῦ ἐσχηκότες. 7 καὶ πορφύραν αὐτὸν περιέβαλον καὶ ἐκά-
θισαν αὐτὸν ἐπὶ καθέδραν κρίσεως λέγοντες· δικαίως κρῖνε,
βασιλεῦ τοῦ Ἰσραήλ. 8 καί τις αὐτῶν ἐνεγκὼν στέφανον
ἀκάνθινον ἔθηκεν ἐπὶ τῆς κεφαλῆς τοῦ κυρίου,
9 καὶ ἕτεροι ἑστῶτες ἐνέπτυον αὐτοῦ ταῖ`ς´ ὄψεσι καὶ
ἄλλοι τὰς σιαγόνας αὐτοῦ ἐράπισαν, ἕτεροι καλάμῳ
ἔνυσσον αὐτὸν καί τινες αὐτὸν ἐμάστιζον λέγοντες·
ταύτῃ τῇ τιμῇ τιμήσωμεν τὸν υἱὸν τοῦ θ(εο)ῦ.

---

3 6 κύριον : κ͞υ ms. ‖ αὐτὸν : αυτων ms. ‖ υἱὸν : ὑιον ms. ‖ 7 περιέβαλον : περιεβαλλον ms. ‖
9 υἱὸν : ὑιον ms.

6 Those who took the Lord ran and pushed him, and they were saying, 'Let us drag around the son of God, now that we have power over him.'

7 They dressed him in purple and made him sit down on a judge's seat as they said, 'Judge justly, King of Israel!' *8* And one of them brought a crown of thorns and put it on the Lord's head. *9* Some stood and spat in his face and others struck his cheeks. Others stabbed him with a reed and certain individuals flogged him as they said, 'Let us honour the son of God with this honour!'

Chapter 4

P. Cair. 10759, page 3, lines 4–15

10 καὶ ἤνεγκον
δύο κακούργους καὶ ἐσταύρωσαν ἀνὰ μέσον αὐτῶν τὸν κ(ύριο)ν·
αὐτὸς δὲ ἐσιώπα ὡς μηδέν<α> πόνον ἔχων. *11* καὶ ὅτε ὤρθω-
σαν τὸν σταυρόν, ἐπέγραψαν ὅτι οὗτός ἐστιν ὁ βασιλεὺς
τοῦ Ἰσραήλ. *12* καὶ τεθεικότες τὰ ἐνδύματα ἔμπροσθεν
αὐτοῦ διεμερίσαντο, καὶ λαχμὸν ἔβαλον ἐπ᾽ αὐτοῖς.
13 εἷς δέ τις τῶν κακούργων ἐκείνων ὠνείδισεν
αὐτοὺς λέγων· ἡμεῖς διὰ τὰ κακὰ ἃ ἐποιήσαμεν οὕτω
πεπόνθαμεν, οὗτος δὲ σωτὴρ γενόμενος τῶν ἀν(θρώπ)ων
τί ἠδίκησεν ὑμᾶς; *14* καὶ ἀγανακτήσαντες ἐπ᾽ αὐτῷ ἐκέ-
λευσαν ἵνα μὴ σκελοκοπηθῇ ὅπως βασανιζόμενος
ἀποθάνῃ.

---

4 11 ὅτε : οτιε ms. ‖ σταυρόν : σταυρων ms. ‖ 13 ὠνείδισεν : ωνειδησεν ms. ‖ οὗτος : ουτως
ms. ‖ ὑμᾶς : ὒμας ms. ‖ 14 ἀποθάνῃ : αποθανοι ms.

10 And they brought two criminals and crucified the Lord between them. But he kept silent as if he had no pain.

11 When they had set the cross upright, they wrote an inscription, 'This is the King of Israel.' *12* And they put his clothes in front of him, divided them up, and cast lots for them.

13 Then one of the criminals denounced them, saying, 'We have suffered in this way because of the bad things we have done, but this man, the one who has become the saviour of humanity – what wrong has he done you?' *14* And they became angry at him and ordered that his legs not be broken so that he would die in torment.

Chapter 5

P.Cair. 10759, page 3, lines 15–18; page 4, lines 1–8

15 ἦν δὲ μεσημβρία, καὶ σκότος κατέσχε
πᾶσαν τὴν Ἰουδαίαν· καὶ ἐθορυβοῦντο καὶ ἠγωνίων
μήποτε ὁ ἥλιος ἔδυ ἐπειδὴ ἔτι ἔζη· γέγραπται <γὰρ> αὐτοῖς
ἥλιον μὴ δῦναι ἐπὶ πεφονευμένῳ. *16* καί τις αὐτῶν
εἶπεν· ποτίσατε αὐτὸν χολὴν μετὰ ὄξους· καὶ κερά-
σαντες ἐπότισαν. *17* καὶ ἐπλήρωσαν πάντα καὶ ἐτε-
λείωσαν κατὰ τῆς κεφαλῆς αὐτῶν τὰ ἁμαρτήμα-
τα. *18* περιήρχοντο δὲ πολλοὶ μετὰ λύχνων ʽνομίζον-
τες ὅτι νύξ ἐστιν ἔπεσάν τε.ʼ *19* καὶ ὁ κ(ύριο)ς ἀνεβόησε
λέγων· ἡ δύναμίς μου, ἡ δύναμις, κατέλειψάς με·
καὶ εἰπὼν ἀνελήφθη. *20* καὶ αὐτῆς ὥρας διεράγη τὸ
καταπέτασμα τοῦ ναοῦ τῆς Ἰερουσαλὴμ εἰς δύο.

---

5 15 πεφονευμένῳ : πεφωνευμενω ms. ‖ 18 νομίζοντες ὅτι νύξ ἐστιν ἔπεσάν τε Robinson[1892]
: νομίζοντες ὅτι νύξ ἐστιν <καὶ> ἐπέσαντο Harnack[1893] : <καὶ> νομίζοντες ὅτι νύξ ἐστιν
ἀνεπαύσαντο Gebhardt[1893] : νομίζοντες ὅτι νύξ ἐστιν ἐσπεύσαντο Bruston[1897] : νομίζοντες
οτι νυξ εστιν επεσαντο (with επε corrected from initially written εσα) ms. ‖ 20 αὐτῆς : αυτος
ms.

15 Then it was noon and darkness came over all Judea. They were distressed and anxious that the sun not set yet because he was still alive; for it is written for them that the sun must not set on one who has been put to death. *16* One of them said, 'Give him gall mixed with vinegar to drink.' And they made the mixture and gave it to him to drink. *17* So they fulfilled everything and brought their sins down on their heads in full.

18 Meanwhile many people were wandering around with lamps because they thought that it was night, and they stumbled about. *19* And the Lord cried out, 'My power, O power, you have abandoned me.' And when he had said this, he was taken up. *20* At that very hour, the curtain of the temple in Jerusalem was torn in two.

Chapter 6

P. Cair. 10759, page 4, lines 9–17

21 καὶ τότε ἀπέσπασαν τοὺς ἥλους ἀπὸ τῶν χειρῶ(ν)
τοῦ κ(υρίο)υ καὶ ἔθηκαν αὐτὸν ἐπὶ τῆς γῆς· καὶ ἡ γῆ πᾶ-
σα ἐσείσθη καὶ φόβος μέγας ἐγένετο. *22* τότε <ὁ> ἥλιος
ἔλαμψε καὶ εὑρέθη ὥρα ἐνάτη. *23* ἐχάρησαν δὲ
οἱ Ἰουδαῖοι καὶ ἔδωκαν τῷ Ἰωσὴφ τὸ σῶμα
αὐτοῦ ἵνα αὐτὸ θάψῃ, ἐπειδὴ θεασάμενος ἦν ὅσ-
α ἀγαθὰ ἐποίησεν. *24* λαβὼν δὲ τὸν κύριον ἔλουσε
καὶ <ἐν>είλησε σινδόνι καὶ εἰσήγαγεν εἰς ἴδιον
τάφον καλούμενον Κῆπον Ἰωσήφ.

---

6 21 ἐγένετο : εγενετο (with final ο corrected from initially written ε) ms. ‖ 23 ἔδωκαν : δεδωκασι ms. ‖ ἵνα : ινι ms. ‖ 24 σινδόνι : σινδονιν ms.

21 Then they pulled the nails out of the Lord's hands and put him on the earth. And the whole earth shook and great fear came over them.

22 Then the sun shone and it was found to be three in the afternoon.†
23 So the Jews rejoiced and gave Joseph his body so that he could bury it (for Joseph‡ had seen all the good things that Jesus‡ had done). 24 Joseph‡ took the Lord, washed him, wrapped him in a linen cloth, and brought him into his own tomb, which is called the Garden of Joseph.

† lit. 'the ninth hour'
‡ lit. 'he'

Chapter 7

P. Cair. 10759, page 4, lines 17–18; page 5, lines 1–9

        25 τότε οἱ Ἰουδαῖοι
καὶ οἱ πρεσβύτεροι καὶ οἱ <ἱ>ερεῖς γνόντες οἷον
κακὸν ἑαυτοῖς ἐποίησαν ἤρξαντο κόπτεσθαι
καὶ λέγειν· οὐαὶ ταῖς ἁμαρτίαις ἡμῶν· ἤγγισεν
ἡ κρίσις καὶ τὸ τέλος Ἰερουσαλήμ. *26* ἐγὼ δὲ μετὰ τῶ(ν)
ἑταίρων μου ἐλυπούμην· καὶ τετρωμένοι κατὰ διάνοιαν ἐκρυβόμεθα· ἐζητούμεθα γὰρ ὑπ᾽ αὐτῶν
ὡς κακοῦργοι καὶ ὡς τὸν ναὸν θέλοντες ἐμπρῆσαι.
27 ἐπὶ δὲ τούτοις πᾶσιν ἐνηστεύομεν καὶ ἐκαθεζόμεθα
πενθοῦντες καὶ κλαίοντες νυκτὸς καὶ ἡμέρας
ἕως τοῦ σαββάτου.

---

7 26 ὑπ᾽ : ϋπ ms.

25 Then the Jews, the elders, and the priests realized what a bad thing they had done to themselves and began to mourn and say, 'Our terrible sins! The judgment and the end of Jerusalem are near.'

26 Meanwhile I was grieving with my friends. We had troubled thoughts and were in hiding. For we were being sought by them as if we were criminals who wanted to set the temple on fire. *27* So we fasted because of all these things, and we sat, mourning and weeping, night and day, until the Sabbath.

Chapter 8

P. Cair. 10759, page 5, lines 9–17; page 6, lines 1–11

    28 συναχθέντες δὲ οἱ γραμματεῖς
καὶ Φαρισαῖοι καὶ πρεσβύτεροι πρὸς ἀλλήλους, ἀκούσαντες ὅτι ὁ λαὸς ἅπας γογγύζει καὶ κόπτεται
τὰ στήθη λέγοντες ὅτι εἰ τῷ θανάτῳ αὐτοῦ ταῦτα τὰ
μέγιστα σημεῖα γέγονεν, ἴδετε ὅτι πόσον δίκαιός
ἐστιν. *29* ἐφοβήθησαν οἱ πρεσβύτεροι καὶ ἦλθον
πρὸς Πειλᾶτον δεόμενοι αὐτοῦ καὶ λέγοντες·
30 παράδος ἡμῖν στρατιώτας ἵνα φυλάξω<σιν> τὸ μνῆμα
αὐτοῦ ἐπὶ τρεῖς ἡμ[έρα]ς, μήποτε ἐλθόντες
οἱ μαθηταὶ αὐτοῦ κλέψωσιν αὐτόν, καὶ ὑπολάβῃ
ὁ λαὸς ὅτι ἐκ νεκρῶν ἀνέστη, καὶ ποιήσωσιν
ἡμῖν κακά. *31* ὁ δὲ Πειλᾶτος παρέδωκεν αὐτοῖς
Πετρώνιον τὸν κεντυρίωνα μετὰ στρατιωτῶν
φυλάσσειν τὸν τάφον. καὶ σὺν αὐτοῖς ἦλθον
πρεσβύτεροι καὶ γραμματεῖς ἐπὶ τὸ μνῆμα. *32* καὶ
κυλίσαντες λίθον μέγαν μετὰ τοῦ κεντυρίωνος
καὶ τῶν στρατιωτῶν ὁμοῦ πάντες οἱ ὄντες ἐκεῖ
ἔθηκαν ἐπὶ τῇ θύρᾳ τοῦ μνήματος, *33* καὶ ἐπέχρισαν
ἑπτὰ σφραγῖδας, καὶ σκηνὴν ἐκεῖ πήξαντες
ἐφύλαξαν.

---

8 30 ἡμέρας Bouriant[1892] ‖ 31 παρέδωκεν : παραδεδωκεν ms. ‖ στρατιωτῶν : στρατιωτον ms.
‖ 32 μετὰ : κατα ms. ‖ 33 ἐπέχρισαν : επεχρεισαν ms.

28 The scribes, Pharisees and elders gathered together when they heard that all the people were grumbling and beating their breasts, saying, 'If these extraordinary signs have happened at his death, you can see how righteous he was.' *29* The elders were afraid and went to Pilate and begged him, *30* 'Give us soldiers to guard his tomb for three days so that his disciples do not come and steal him. Otherwise the people may assume that he has risen from the dead, and they will do bad things to us.'

31 So Pilate gave them the centurion Petronius and soldiers to guard the tomb, and elders and scribes went with them to the tomb. *32* Everyone who was there helped the centurion and the soldiers roll a large stone and put it at the entrance of the tomb. *33* They smeared seven wax seals on the entrance. Then they pitched a tent there and kept guard.

Chapter 9

P. Cair. 10759, page 6, lines 11–17; page 7, lines 1–5

34 πρωῒας δὲ ἐπιφώσκοντος τοῦ σαββάτου, ἦλθεν ὄχλος ἀπὸ Ἰερουσαλὴμ καὶ τῆς περι-
χώρου ἵνα ἴδωσι τὸ μνημεῖον ἐσφραγισμένο(ν).
35 τῇ δὲ νυκτὶ ᾗ ἐπέφωσκεν ἡ κυριακὴ φυλασσόν-
των τῶν στρατιωτῶν ἀνὰ δύο δύο κατὰ φρουρά(ν),
μεγάλη φωνὴ ἐγένετο ἐν τῷ οὐρανῷ. *36* καὶ εἶδο(ν)
ἀνοιχθέντας τοὺς οὐραγοὺς καὶ δύο ἄνδρας
κατελθόντας ἐκεῖθε<ν>, πολὺ φέγγος ἔχοντας
καὶ ἐγγίσαντας τῷ τάφῳ. *37* ὁ δὲ λίθος ἐκεῖνος
ὁ βεβλημένος ἐπὶ τῇ θύρᾳ ἀφ᾽ ἑαυτοῦ κυλισθεὶς
ἐπεχώρησε παρὰ μέρος· καὶ ὁ τάφος ἠνοίγη
καὶ ἀμφότεροι οἱ νεανίσκοι εἰσῆλθον.

9 36 ἀνοιχθέντας : ανοιχθεντες ms. ‖ 37 λίθος : λειθος ms. ‖ ἠνοίγη : ενοιγη ms.

34 Now when the Sabbath morning dawned, a crowd came from Jerusalem and the surrounding region to see that the tomb had been sealed. *35* Then during the night on which the Lord's day dawned, while the soldiers were keeping guard two by two in every watch, a great voice came from the sky. *36* And they saw the skies open; two men, who were magnificently illuminated, came down and approached the tomb. *37* Then the stone that had been put at the entrance rolled by itself and moved partially to the side. The tomb was opened and both the young men went in.

Chapter 10

P. Cair. 10759, page 7, lines 5–16

38 ἰδόντες
οὖν οἱ στρατιῶται ἐκεῖνοι ἐξύπνισαν τὸν κεντυρίωνα καὶ τοὺς πρεσβυτέρους – παρῆσαν γὰρ καὶ αὐτοὶ
φυλάσσοντες – *39* καὶ ἐξηγουμένων αὐτῶν ἃ εἶδον,
πάλιν ὁρῶσιν ἐξελθόντας ἀπὸ τοῦ τάφου τρεῖς
ἄνδρας, καὶ τοὺς δύο τὸν ἕνα ὑπορθοῦντας καὶ
σταυρὸν ἀκολο<υ>θοῦντα αὐτοῖς· *40* καὶ τῶν μὲν δύο
τὴν κεφαλὴν χωροῦσαν μέχρι τοῦ οὐρανοῦ,
τοῦ δὲ χειραγωγουμένου ὑπ' αὐτῶν ὑπερβαίνου-
σαν τοὺς οὐρανούς· *41* καὶ φωνῇ<ς> ἤκουον ἐκ τῶν
οὐρανῶν λεγούσης· ἐκήρυξας τοῖς κοιμωμένοις;
42 καὶ ὑπακοὴ ἠκούετο ἀπὸ τοῦ σταυροῦ <ὅ>τι ναί.

---

10 39 ὁρῶσιν ἐξελθόντας ἀπὸ τοῦ τάφου τρεῖς ἄνδρας : ορασιν εξελθοντος απο του ταφου τρεις ανδρες ms. ‖ 40 χειραγωγουμένου : χειρατωτουμενου ms. ‖ 41 κοιμωμένοις : κοινωμενοις ms. ‖ 42 ὅτι ναί Harnack[1893] : τὸ ναί Swete[1892] : τιναι ms.

38 When the soldiers saw, they woke the centurion and the elders (for they were also there keeping guard). *39* But while they were explaining what they had seen, they saw three men come out of the tomb again. Two of them were supporting the third and a cross was following them. *40* The heads of the two reached as far as the sky, but the head of the one being hand-led by them extended beyond the skies. *41* And they heard a voice from the skies which said, 'Did you preach to those who sleep?'

42 And an answer was heard from the cross, 'Yes.'

Chapter 11

P. Cair. 10759, page 7, lines 16–17; page 8, lines 1–15

43 συνε-
σκέπτοντο οὖν ἀλλήλοις ἐκεῖνοι ἀπελθεῖν
καὶ ἐνφανίσαι ταῦτα τῷ Πειλάτῳ· *44* καὶ ἔτι διανοουμέ(ν)-
ων αὐτῶν φαίνονται πάλιν ἀνοιχθέντες οἱ οὐρανοὶ
καὶ ἄν(θρωπ)ός τις κατελθὼν καὶ εἰσελθὼν εἰς τὸ μνῆμα.
45 ταῦτα ἰδόντες οἱ περὶ τὸν κεντυρ<ί>ωνα νυκτὸς ἔσπευσαν
πρὸς Πειλᾶτον, ἀφέντες τὸν τάφον ὃν ἐφύλασσον· καὶ
ἐξηγήσαντο πάντα ἅπερ εἶδον, ἀγωνιῶντες μεγάλως
καὶ λέγοντες· ἀληθῶς υἱὸς ἦν θ(εο)ῦ. *46* ἀποκριθεὶς ὁ Πειλᾶτος
ἔφη· ἐγὼ καθαρεύω τοῦ αἵματος τοῦ υἱοῦ τοῦ θεοῦ, ὑμῖν δὲ
τοῦτο ἔδοξεν. *47* εἶτα προσελθόντες πάντες ἐδέοντο αὐτοῦ
καὶ παρεκάλουν κελεῦσαι τῷ κεντυρίων<ι> καὶ τοῖς στρατιώταις μηδὲν εἰπεῖν ἃ εἶδον· *48* συμφέρει γάρ, φασίν, ἡμῖν
ὀφλῆσαι μεγίστην ἁμαρτίαν ἔμπροσθεν τοῦ θεοῦ
καὶ μὴ ἐμπεσεῖν εἰς χεῖρας τοῦ λαοῦ τῶν Ἰουδαίων
καὶ λιθασθῆναι. *49* ἐκέλευσεν οὖν ὁ Πειλᾶτος τῷ κεντυρίωνι καὶ τοῖς στρατιώταις μηδὲν εἰπεῖν.

---

11 44 κατελθὼν : κατελθον ms. ‖ 45 ἀγωνιῶντες : απανιωντες ms. ‖ υἱὸς : υιος ms. ‖ 46 υἱοῦ : ϋιου ms. ‖ ὑμῖν : ημιν ms. ‖ 47 παρεκάλουν : περεκαλουν ms. ‖ 48 ἐμπεσεῖν : εμπεσειν (with σ corrected from initially written τ) ms. ‖ 49 τῷ κεντυρίωνι : των κεντυριων ms.

43 So they decided together to go and inform Pilate about these things. *44* But while they were still considering matters, the skies appeared to open again, and a man came down and went into the tomb. *45* When the centurion and those who were with him saw these things, they left the tomb they were guarding and hurried off to Pilate during the night. And they explained everything they had seen and said with great anxiety, 'He truly was the son of God!'

46 Pilate answered, 'I am clean from the blood of the son of God. You are the ones who thought this best.'

47 Then everybody came and begged him, and they urged him to order the centurion and the soldiers not to say anything about what they had seen. *48* 'For it is better for us,' they said, 'to be guilty of a most grievous sin before God than to fall into the hands of the Jewish people and be stoned.' *49* So Pilate ordered the centurion and the soldiers not to say anything.

Chapter 12

P. Cair. 10759, page 8, lines 15–17; page 9, lines 1–14

50 ὄρθ<ρ>ου δὲ
τῆς κυριακῆς Μαριὰμ ἡ Μαγδαληνή, μαθήτρια τοῦ κ(υρίο)υ –
φοβουμένη διὰ τοὺς Ἰουδαίους, ἐπειδὴ ἐφλέγοντο
ὑπὸ τῆς ὀργῆς, οὐκ ἐποίησεν ἐπὶ τῷ μνήματι τοῦ κ(υρίο)υ
ἃ εἰώθεσαν ποιεῖν αἱ γυναῖκες ἐπὶ τοῖς ἀποθνήσκουσι
καὶ τοῖς ἀγαπωμένοις αὐταῖς – 51 λαβοῦσα μεθ᾽ ἑαυτῆς τὰς φίλας
ἦλθε<ν> ἐπὶ τὸ μνημεῖον ὅπου ἦν τεθείς. 52 καὶ ἐφοβοῦντο
μὴ ἴδωσιν αὐτὰς οἱ Ἰουδαῖοι καὶ ἔλεγον· εἰ καὶ μὴ ἐν ἐ-
κείνῃ τῇ ἡμέρᾳ ᾗ ἐσταυρώθη ἐδυνήθημεν κλαῦσαι
καὶ κόψασθαι, κἂν νῦν ἐπὶ τοῦ μνήματος αὐτοῦ ποιήσωμε(ν)
ταῦτα. 53 τίς δὲ ἀποκυλίσει ἡμῖν καὶ τὸν λίθον τὸν τεθέντα
ἐπὶ τῆς θύρας τοῦ μνημείου ἵνα εἰσελθοῦσαι παρακαθεσ-
θῶμεν αὐτῷ καὶ ποιήσωμεν τὰ ὀφ<ε>ιλόμενα; 54 μέγας γὰρ
ἦν ὁ λίθος, καὶ φοβούμεθα μή τις ἡμᾶς ἴδῃ. καὶ εἰ μὴ δυ-
νάμεθα, κἂν ἐπὶ τῆς θύρας βάλωμεν ἃ φέρομεν εἰς
μνημοσύνην αὐτοῦ, κλαύσομεν καὶ κοψόμεθα ἕως
ἔλθωμεν εἰς τὸν οἶκον ἡμῶν.

12 50 Μαριὰμ ἡ Μαγδαληνή : μαριαμ᾽ η μαγδαλινη ms. ‖ 52 κόψασθαι : κοψεσθαι ms. ‖
κἂν : και ms.

50 Now Mary Magdalene, a disciple of the Lord, did not immediately do at the Lord's tomb what women customarily do for those who die and are beloved to them. She had been afraid of the Jews because they were inflamed with anger.

But at dawn on the Lord's day, *51* she took her friends with her and went to the tomb where he had been put. *52* And they were afraid that the Jews might see them and they said, 'Even though we could not weep and mourn on the day he was crucified, we may now do these things at his tomb. *53* But who will roll away the stone that was put at the entrance of the tomb for us so that we can go in, sit with him, and do the things that we should? *54* For the stone was large, and we are afraid that someone may see us. Nevertheless, if we are not able to go in, we may place the things we have brought at the entrance as a memorial for him. We will weep and mourn until we go to our houses.'

Chapter 13

P. Cair. 10759, page 9, lines 14–17; page 10, lines 1–6

55 καὶ ἀπελθοῦσαι εὗρον
τὸν τάφον ἠνεῳγμένον· καὶ προσελθοῦσαι παρέκυ-
ψαν ἐκεῖ, καὶ ὁρῶσιν ἐκεῖ τινα νεανίσκον καθεζό-
μενον <ἐν> μέσῳ τοῦ τάφου ὡραῖον καὶ περιβεβλημένο(ν)
στολὴν λαμπροτάτην, ὅστις ἔφη αὐταῖς· 56 τί ἤλθα-
τε; τίνα ζητεῖτε; μὴ τὸν σταυρωθέντα ἐκεῖνον;
ἀνέστη καὶ ἀπῆλθεν· εἰ δὲ μὴ πιστεύετε, παρακύ-
ψατε καὶ ἴδετε τὸν τόπον ἔνθα ἔκειʼτοʼ, ὅτι οὐκ ἔστιν·
ἀνέστη γὰρ καὶ ἀπῆλθεν ἐκεῖ ὅθεν ἀπεστάλη.
57 τότε αἱ γυναῖκες φοβηθεῖσ<αι> ἔφυγον.

---

13 55 αὐταῖς : αυταιο ms. ‖ 56 πιστεύετε : πιστευεται ms. ‖ ἴδετε : ιδατε ms.

55 So they went and found that the tomb had been opened. When they came to it, they stooped down and saw a young man sitting there in the middle of the tomb. He was beautiful and dressed in an extraordinarily radiant robe. He said to them, 56 'Why have you come? Whom are you seeking? Not the one who was crucified? He has risen and gone out. If you do not believe, stoop down and see the place where he lay, that he is not there. For he has risen and gone out to the place from which he was sent.'

57 Then the women were frightened and fled.

Chapter 14

P. Cair. 10759, page 10, lines 6–14

58 ἦν δὲ τελευταία
ἡμέρα τῶν ἀζύμων, καὶ πολλοί τινες ἐξήρχοντο
ὑποστρέφοντες εἰς τοὺς οἴκους αὐτῶν τῆς ἑορτῆς
παυσαμένης. *59* ἡμεῖς δὲ οἱ δώδεκα μαθηταὶ τοῦ κ(υρίο)υ
ἐκλαίομεν καὶ ἐλυπούμεθα, καὶ ἕκαστος λυπούμενος
διὰ τὸ συμβὰν ἀπηλλάγη εἰς τὸν οἶκον αὐτοῦ. *60* ἐγὼ δὲ
Σίμων Πέτρος καὶ Ἀνδρέας ὁ ἀδελφός μου λαβόντες ἡμῶν τὰ λίνα ἀπήλθαμεν εἰς τὴν θάλ-
ασσαν· καὶ ἦν σὺν ἡμῖν Λευεὶς ὁ τοῦ Ἀλφαίου, ὃν <ὁ> κ(ύριο)ς . . .

---

14 *58* ὑποστρέφοντες : ὑποστρεφοντες ms. ‖ παυσαμένης : παυσαμινης ms. ‖ *60* θάλασσαν :
θαλλασσαν ms.

58 Now it was the last day of the Feast of Unleavened Bread, and many were setting out to return to their houses because the feast had ended. *59* We, the twelve disciples of the Lord, were weeping and grieving. And each one departed to his house, grieving because of what had happened. *60* My brother Andrew and I, Simon Peter, took our fishing nets and went out to the sea. And with us was Levi, the son of Alphaeus, whom the Lord . . .

Oxyrhynchus Papyrus 2949

P.Oxy. 2949, fragment 1

].[

]ν.. [

εἱστήκει δὲ ἐκεῖ]
5 ['Ιωσήφ,] ὁ φίλος Π[ε]ιλά[τ]ου κ[αὶ τοῦ κ(υρίο)υ,]
[καὶ εἰδ]ὼς ὅτι ἐκέλευσεν [σταυρωθ-]
[ῆναι ἐλ]θὼν πρὸς Πειλᾶτο[ν ᾔτησεν]
[τοῦ κ(υρίο)υ] τ[ὸ] σῶμα εἰς ταφήν. [Πειλᾶτος]
[πέμψας πρὸς Ἡρῴδ]ην ᾔτήσα[το αὐτῷ]
10 [τὸ σῶμα ἀποδοθ]ῆναι εἰπώ[ν·
] ᾔτήσατ[ο
] αὐτόν [
]. ὅτι α[

P.Oxy. 2949, fragment 2

. μου[
Πειλ[ᾶτε, ἀδελφέ μου, εἰ καὶ μή]
3 τις α[ὐτὸν ᾔτήκει, ἡμεῖς ἐθάπτο-]
μεγ [αὐτόν

Lost text on P.Oxy. 2949 has been restored so that it corresponds as closely as possible with *Gos. Pet.* 2.3–5 on P.Cair. 10759. However, it should be noted that the accuracy of the restorations is extremely uncertain because P.Oxy. 2949 and P.Cair. 10759 apparently contained different versions of the *Gospel of Peter.*

---

1 4 εἱστήκει δὲ ἐκεῖ Lührmann[2000] ‖ 5 'Ιωσήφ Lührmann[1981] ‖ Πειλάτου καὶ τοῦ κυρίου Coles[1972] ‖ 6 καὶ εἰδὼς Lührmann[2000] : εἰδώις Coles[1972] : [ειδ]ωις pap. ‖ σταυρωθῆναι Lührmann[2000] ‖ 7 ἐλθὼν Coles[1972] ‖ ᾔτησεν Lührmann[1981] ‖ 8 τοῦ κυρίου Bernhard ‖ Πειλᾶτος πέμψας πρὸς Lührmann[2000] ‖ 9 Ἡρῴδην ᾔτήσατο Coles[1972] ‖ αὐτῷ τὸ σῶμα Lührmann[2000] ‖ 10 ἀποδοθῆναι Coles[1972]
2 2 Πειλᾶτε, ἀδελφέ . . . (3) ἐθάπτομεν αὐτὸν Bernhard

... εἰστήκει δὲ ἐκεῖ Ἰωσήφ, ὁ φίλος Πειλάτου καὶ τοῦ κυρίου, καὶ εἰδὼς ὅτι ἐκέλευσεν σταυρωθῆναι ἐλθὼν πρὸς Πειλᾶτον ᾔτησεν τοῦ κυρίου τὸ σῶμα εἰς ταφήν. Πειλᾶτος πέμψας πρὸς Ἡρῴδην ᾐτήσατο αὐτῷ τὸ σῶμα ἀποδοθῆναι εἰπών ... ᾐτήσατο ... αὐτόν ... ὅτι ...

... Now Joseph, the friend of Pilate and of the Lord, had been standing there. When he realized that he had ordered him crucified, he came to Pilate and asked for the Lord's body for burial. Pilate sent to Herod and asked for the body to be returned to him, saying ... asked for ... him ... that ...

... Πειλᾶτε, ἀδελφέ μου, εἰ καὶ μή τις αὐτὸν ᾐτήκει, ἡμεῖς ἐθάπτομεν αὐτόν ...

... Pilate, my brother, even if nobody had asked for him, we would have buried him ...

EGERTON PAPYRUS 2: THE UNKNOWN GOSPEL

When H. I. Bell and T. C. Skeat published the first modern edition of Egerton Papyrus 2 (P.Egerton 2) in 1935, they gave the text preserved on the newly recovered manuscript an appropriate title: the *Unknown Gospel*. The manuscript itself had been acquired by the British Museum the previous year, but the dealer who had sold it to the museum could not (or would not) provide any information about where it had been found. The part of the manuscript that would have contained the ancient title of the gospel had been lost. The identity of the gospel could not be discovered and neither could any trace of its use in antiquity. Practically everything about the gospel seemed 'unknown'.

Nonetheless, the publication of the *Unknown Gospel* caused quite a stir. At the time of its discovery, P.Egerton 2 was 'unquestionably the earliest specifically Christian manuscript yet discovered'.[1] Additionally, after carefully examining the text itself, Bell and Skeat concluded that 'the evidence indicates rather strongly that it represents a source or sources independent of those used by the Synoptic Gospels . . . Its relation to John is such as to suggest for serious consideration the question whether it may be, or derive from, a source used by that Gospel'.[2] The early date of the manuscript combined with the assertions of Bell and Skeat (which are still debated to this day) were more than enough to excite the interest of both scholars and the general public.

Although the *Unknown Gospel* remains somewhat mysterious, our knowledge of the text has been improved slightly since the initial discovery of P.Egerton 2. Thanks to the keen eye of Michael Gronewald, an additional piece of the same manuscript has been identified among the Cologne papyri. P.Köln 255, which contains roughly ten additional lines from the bottom of fragment 1 of P.Egerton 2, was published in 1987.

1. H. I. Bell and T. C. Skeat, *Fragments of an Unknown Gospel and Other Early Christian Papyri* (London: Oxford University Press, 1935), p. 1. Although P.Ryl. 457 ($\mathfrak{P}52$) is now generally recognized as the earliest Christian manuscript (ca. 125 CE), P.Egerton 2 is still one of the earliest. For information on P.Ryl. 457, which was published shortly after P.Egerton 2 in 1935, see C. H. Roberts (ed.), *An Unpublished Fragment of the Fourth Gospel in the John Rylands Library* (Manchester: Manchester University Press, 1935).
2. Bell and Skeat, *Fragments of an Unknown Gospel*, p. 38.

The *Unknown Gospel* was a narrative gospel similar to Matthew, Mark, Luke and John. The part of the gospel that has been preserved describes the activities and teachings of Jesus during his earthly ministry. The text seems to anticipate a passion narrative, but it is impossible to know what else the gospel included.[3] The *Unknown Gospel*'s closest parallels are with John, but it also contains an otherwise unattested miracle story and passages that resemble parts of Matthew, Mark and Luke.

A bewildering assortment of systems of notation have been used with the *Unknown Gospel* because pieces of the manuscript were discovered at different times and because scholars have disagreed about the order in which the leaves from the codex are to be read.[4] For the present edition, it has seemed best simply to divide the text on the basis of natural manuscript divisions (i.e., page breaks) and refrain from adding any additional notation. The order of the leaves proposed by the original editors has been retained, even though it is not certainly correct.[5]

Egerton Papyrus 2 (*P.Egerton 2*)

Contents: 1. A dispute about the authority of Jesus in which Jesus declares that Moses and the scriptures testify about him (cf. Jn 5.39; 5.45; 9.29; 5.46); 2. The end of an incident in which the rulers seek to have Jesus

---

3. P.Egerton 2, fragment 1(→).7–8 seems to foreshadow a passion narrative with the statement, 'The hour of his arrest had not yet come.'

4. Each of the following major publications uses a different system of notation for the *Unknown Gospel*: Bell and Skeat, *Fragments of an Unknown Gospel*, pp. 9–15; H. I. Bell and T. C. Skeat, *The New Gospel Fragments* (London: Oxford University Press, 1935), pp. 29–32; M. Gronewald, '255. Unbekanntes Evangelium oder Evangelienharmonie (Fragment aus dem "Evangelium Egerton")', in vol. 6 of *Kölner Papyri (P.Köln)* (eds. M. Gronewald, B. Kramer, K. Maresch, M. Parca and C. Römer; Opladen, Germany: Westdeutscher Verlag, 1987), pp. 136–45 (139–42); J. B. Daniels, 'The Egerton Gospel: Its Place in Early Christianity' (unpublished doctoral dissertation; Claremont Graduate School, 1990), pp. 12–21; R. J. Miller (ed.), *The Complete Gospels: Annotated Scholars Version* (Sonoma, CA: Polebridge Press, rev. and exp. edn, 1994), pp. 414–17; D. Lührmann and E. Schlarb, *Fragmente apokryph gewordener Evangelien in griechischer und lateinischer Sprache* (Marburger theologische Studien, 59; Marburg, Germany: N.G. Elwert Verlag, 2000), pp. 145–53; B. D. Ehrman, *Lost Scriptures: Books That Did Not Make It into the New Testament* (New York: Oxford University Press, 2003), p. 30.

5. There is a general consensus that P.Egerton 2, fragment 1(↓) preceded 1(→) because the first eight lines of 1(→) appear to continue the narrative from 1(↓), but the order of fragments 2 and 3 has been disputed. Bell and Skeat arranged the fragments: 1(↓), 1(→), 2(→), 2(↓), 3(↓), 3(→). For their justification, see Bell and Skeat, *Fragments of an Unknown Gospel*, pp. 39–41. Gallizia proposed that the fragments should be ordered: 1(↓), 1(→), 3(→), 3(↓), 2(↓), 2(→) or 1(↓), 1(→), 3(↓), 3(→), 2(↓), 2(→). For his justification, see U. Gallizia, 'Il P. Egerton 2', *Aeg* 36 (1956), pp. 29–72, 178–234 (46–47). Arguments for both arrangements are highly speculative; the order of these two fragments should be considered uncertain.

stoned (cf. Jn 8.59; 7.30) followed by the healing of a leper (cf. Mt. 8.1–4; Mk 1.40–45; Lk. 5.12–16); 3. A question about paying tribute to rulers (cf. Jn 3.2; Mt. 22.15–22; Mk 12.13–17; Lk. 20.20–26) that Jesus answers by quoting the prophet Isaiah (cf. Mt. 15.7–9; Mk 7.6–7); 4. An otherwise unknown miracle of Jesus.

Date copied: Middle of second century (Bell and Skeat).
Late second or early third century (Gronewald).

Basic Description: Papyrus codex; three leaves (two mostly preserved), w. 9.2 x h. 11.5 cm (fragment 1), w. 9.7 x h. 11.8 cm (fragment 2), w. 2.3 x h. 6.0 cm (fragment 3); 92 mostly preserved lines of text (with 10 largely from P.Köln 255).

Nomina sacra: Probably β̄αλευσιν (βασιλεῦσιν); probably η̄σας (Ἡσαΐας); θ̄ς (θεός); probably θ̄υ (θεοῦ); ῑη (Ἰησοῦς, Ἰησοῦ); κ̄ς (κύριος); μ̄ω (Μωϋσῆς, Μωϋσεῖ); π̄ρα (πατέρα); probably επροφσεν (ἐπροφήτευσεν); προφας (προφήτας).

Other notable features: Punctuation in the form of frequent high points and as small blank space at the ends of sentences; letters following punctuation often enlarged, especially epsilon; some final nus suppressed, indicated by a supralinear stroke over the preceding letter.

Current housing location: British Library, London.

Museum ID: Egerton Papyrus 2.

First published edition + colour manuscript photos: H. I. Bell and T. C. Skeat, *Fragments of an Unknown Gospel and Other Early Christian Papyri* (London: Oxford University Press, 1935).

Revision of first published edition: H. I. Bell and T. C. Skeat, *The New Gospel Fragments* (London: Oxford University Press, 1935).

Cologne Papyrus 255 (P.Köln 255)

Basic Description: Papyrus codex; one fragment, w. 6.5 x h. 3.0 cm; 10 lines of text (5 lines from the bottom of each side of fragment 1 of P.Egerton 2).

Nomina sacra: None visible.

Other notable features: Apostrophe between one pair of consonants.

Current housing location: Institut für Altertumskunde, Universität zu Köln (Institute for Archaeology, University of Cologne).

Museum ID: Inv. Nr. 608.

First published edition (official publication): M. Gronewald, '255. Unbekanntes Evangelium oder Evangelienharmonie (Fragment aus dem "Evangelium Egerton")', in vol. 6 of *Kölner Papyri (P.Köln)* (eds. M. Gronewald, B. Kramer, K. Maresch, M. Parca and C. Römer; Opladen, Germany: Westdeutscher Verlag, 1987), pp. 136–45.

Other important editions

Critical edition of P.Egerton 2 without P.Köln 255: G. Mayeda, *Das Leben-Jesu-Fragment: Papyrus Egerton 2 und seine Stellung in der urchristlichen Literaturgeschichte* (Bern: Verlag Paul Haupt, 1946).

Critical edition of P.Egerton 2 with P.Köln 255: J. B. Daniels, 'The Egerton Gospel: Its Place in Early Christianity'(unpublished doctoral dissertation; Claremont Graduate School, 1990).

Egerton Papyrus 2 with Cologne Papyrus 255

P.Egerton 2, fragment 1 + P.Köln 255(↓)

```
                    ] μ[
          ] τοῖ[ς] νομικο[ῖς
       ]ντα τὸν παραπράσσ[οντα]
       ]μον καὶ μὴ ἐμέ· . [ . . ] . . . .
5      ] ι ὃ ποιεῖ πῶς ποιε[ῖ·] πρὸς
   [δὲ τοὺς] ἄ[ρ]χοντας τοῦ λαοῦ [στ]ρα-
   [φεὶς εἶ]πεν τὸν λόγον τοῦτο[ν·] ἐραυ-
   [νᾶτε τ]ὰς γραφάς, ἐν αἷς ὑμεῖς δο-
   [κεῖτε] ζωὴν ἔχειν· ἐκεῖναί εἰ[σ]ιν
10 [αἱ μαρτ]υροῦσαι περὶ ἐμοῦ· μὴ 'γ[ο-]
   [μίζετε ὅ]τι` ἐγὼ ἦλθον κατηγο[ρ]ῆσαι
   [ὑμῶν] πρὸς τὸν π(ατέ)ρα μου· ἔστιν
   [ὁ κατη]γορῶν ὑμῶν Μω(ϋσῆς), εἰς ὃν
   [ὑμεῖς] ἠλπίκατε. α[ὐ]τῶν δὲ λε-
15 [γόντω]ν ε[ὖ] οἴδαμεν ὅτι Μω(ϋσεῖ) ἐλά-
   [λησεν] ὁ θ(εό)ς, σὲ δὲ οὐκ οἴδαμεν
   [πόθεν εἶ.] ἀποκριθεὶς ὁ Ἰη(σοῦς) εἶ-
   [πεν αὐτο]ῖς· νῦν κατηγορεῖται
   [ὑμῶν τὸ ἀ]πιστεῖ[ν] τοῖς ὑπ᾿ αὐτοῦ
20 [μεμαρτυρη]μέγοις· εἰ γὰρ ἐπι-
   [στεύσατε Μω(ϋσεῖ),] ἐπιστεύσατε ἂ[ν]
   [ἐμοί· πε]ρ[ὶ] ἐμοῦ γὰρ ἐκεῖνο[ς]
   [ἔγραψε]ν τοῖς πατ[ρά]σιν ὑμῶ[ν.]
                    ]ε[
```

1(↓) 5 ποιεῖ· πρὸς . . . (10) αἱ μαρτυροῦσαι Bell-Skeat[1935a] ‖ 8 ὑμεῖς : ῡμεις pap. ‖ 10 νομίζετε ὅτι Gronewald[1987] : δοκεῖτε ὅτι Bell-Skeat[1935a] ‖ 11 κατηγορῆσαι ὑμῶν . . . (18) κατηγορεῖται ὑμῶν Bell-Skeat[1935a] ‖ 13 ὑμῶν : ῡμων pap. ‖ 19 τὸ ἀπιστεῖν . . . (23) πατράσιν ὑμῶν Gronewald[1987]

... τοῖς νομικοῖς ... τὸν παραπράσσοντα ... καὶ μὴ ἐμέ ... ὃ ποιεῖ πῶς ποιεῖ· πρὸς δὲ τοὺς ἄρχοντας τοῦ λαοῦ στραφεὶς εἶπεν τὸν λόγον τοῦτον· ἐραυνᾶτε τὰς γραφάς, ἐν αἷς ὑμεῖς δοκεῖτε ζωὴν ἔχειν· ἐκεῖναί εἰσιν αἱ μαρτυροῦσαι περὶ ἐμοῦ· μὴ νομίζετε ὅτι ἐγὼ ἦλθον κατηγορῆσαι ὑμῶν πρὸς τὸν πατέρα μου· ἔστιν ὁ κατηγορῶν ὑμῶν Μωϋσῆς, εἰς ὃν ὑμεῖς ἠλπίκατε. αὐτῶν δὲ λεγόντων εὖ οἴδαμεν ὅτι Μωϋσεῖ ἐλάλησεν ὁ θεός, σὲ δὲ οὐκ οἴδαμεν πόθεν εἶ. ἀποκριθεὶς ὁ Ἰησοῦς εἶπεν αὐτοῖς· νῦν κατηγορεῖται ὑμῶν τὸ ἀπιστεῖν τοῖς ὑπ᾽ αὐτοῦ μεμαρτυρημένοις· εἰ γὰρ ἐπιστεύσατε Μωϋσεῖ, ἐπιστεύσατε ἂν ἐμοί· περὶ ἐμοῦ γὰρ ἐκεῖνος ἔγραψεν τοῖς πατράσιν ὑμῶν ...

'. . . to the lawyers . . . the one who acts unjustly . . . and not me . . . how he does what he does.'

Then he turned to the rulers of the people and made this statement, 'Search the scriptures; you suppose that you have life in them. It is they that bear witness about me. Do not think that I have come to accuse you to my father. There is one who accuses you: Moses, on whom you have set your hope.'

They said, 'We know well that God spoke to Moses, but as for you, we do not know where you are from.'

Jesus answered them, 'You now stand accused because of your failure to believe those who have been approved by him. For if you believed Moses, you would believe me; for he wrote about me to your fathers . . .'

P.Egerton 2, fragment 1 + P.Köln 255(→)

```
           ] . λω[ . . . . ] . [
        ] λίθους ὁμοῦ λι[θάσω-]
     σι[ν αὐ]τόν· καὶ ἐπέβαλον [τὰς]
     χεῖ[ρας] αὐτῶν ἐπ᾽ αὐτὸν οἱ [ἄρχον-]
5    τες [ἵν]α πιάσωσιν καὶ παρ[αδῶσιν]
     αὐ[τὸ]ν τῷ ὄχλῳ· καὶ οὐκ ἠ[δύναντο]
     αὐτὸν πιάσαι, ὅτι οὔπω ἐ[ληλύθει]
     αὐτοῦ ἡ ὥρα τῆς παραδό[σεως.]
     [αὐ]τὸς δὲ ὁ κ(ύριο)ς ἐξελθὼν [ἐκ τῶν χει-]
10   ρῶν ἀπένευσεν ἀπ᾽[αὐτῶν.]
     κα[ὶ ἰ]δοὺ λεπρὸς προσελθ[ὼν αὐτῷ]
     λέγει· διδάσκαλε Ἰη(σοῦ), λε[προῖς συν-]
     οδεύων καὶ συνεσθίω[ν αὐτοῖς]
     ἐν τῷ πανδοχείῳ ἐλ[έπρησα]
15   καὶ αὐτὸς ἐγώ· ἐὰν [ο]ὖν [σὺ θέλῃς,]
     καθαρίζομαι. ὁ δὲ κ(ύριο)ς [ἔφη αὐτῷ·]
     θέλ[ω], καθαρίσθητι. [καὶ εὐθέως]
     [ἀ]πέστη ἀπ᾽ αὐτοῦ ἡ λέπ[ρα· λέγει]
     δὲ αὐτῷ ὁ Ἰη(σοῦς)· πορε[υθεὶς σεαυ-]
20   τὸν ἐπίδειξον τοῖ[ς ἱερεῦσιν]
     καὶ ἀνένεγκον [περὶ τοῦ κα-]
     [θ]αρισμοῦ ὡς ἐπ[έταξεν Μω(ϋσῆς) καὶ]
     [μ]ηκέτι ἀ[μά]ρτανε [ . . . . . . ] . . [
```

1(→) 2 λιθάσωσιν αὐτόν . . . (4) ἄρχοντες ἵνα Bell-Skeat[1935a] ‖ 5 παραδῶσιν αὐτὸν van Groningen[1935] : παραδώσωσιν Bell-Skeat[1935b] ‖ 6 ἠδύναντο Bell-Skeat[1935b] : ἐδύναντο Bell-Skeat[1935a] ‖ 7 ἐληλύθει Bell-Skeat[1935a] ‖ 8 παραδόσεως αὐτὸς Bell-Skeat[1935a] ‖ 9 ἐκ τῶν χείρων Bell-Skeat[1935b] ‖ 10 αὐτῶν καί . . . (18) ἡ λέπρα Bell-Skeat[1935a] ‖ 16 δὲ : δη pap. ‖ 18 λέγει δὲ . . . (21) τοῦ καθαρισμοῦ Gronewald[1987] ‖ 21 ἀνένεγκον : ανενεγ᾽κον pap. ‖ 22 ὡς ἐπ[έταξεν] Bernhard : ως επ[εταξεν] pap. ‖ Μωϋσῆς καὶ μηκέτι ἁμάρτανε Gronewald[1987]

... λίθους ὁμοῦ λιθάσωσιν αὐτόν· καὶ ἐπέβαλον τὰς χεῖρας αὐτῶν ἐπ'
αὐτὸν οἱ ἄρχοντες ἵνα πιάσωσιν καὶ παραδῶσιν αὐτὸν τῷ ὄχλῳ· καὶ οὐκ
ἠδύναντο αὐτὸν πιάσαι, ὅτι οὔπω ἐληλύθει αὐτοῦ ἡ ὥρα τῆς παραδόσεως.
αὐτὸς δὲ ὁ κύριος ἐξελθὼν ἐκ τῶν χειρῶν ἀπένευσεν ἀπ' αὐτῶν. καὶ ἰδοὺ
λεπρὸς προσελθὼν αὐτῷ λέγει· διδάσκαλε Ἰησοῦ, λεπροῖς συνοδεύων
καὶ συνεσθίων αὐτοῖς ἐν τῷ πανδοχείῳ ἐλέπρησα καὶ αὐτὸς ἐγώ· ἐὰν οὖν
σὺ θέλῃς, καθαρίζομαι. ὁ δὲ κύριος ἔφη αὐτῷ· θέλω, καθαρίσθητι. καὶ
εὐθέως ἀπέστη ἀπ' αὐτοῦ ἡ λέπρα· λέγει δὲ αὐτῷ ὁ Ἰησοῦς· πορευθεὶς
σεαυτὸν ἐπίδειξον τοῖς ἱερεῦσιν καὶ ἀνένεγκον περὶ τοῦ καθαρισμοῦ ὡς
ἐπέταξεν Μωϋσῆς καὶ μηκέτι ἁμάρτανε ...

... stones together so that they could stone him. The rulers were trying to
lay their hands on him so that they could seize him and deliver him to the
crowd. But they could not seize him because the hour of his arrest had not
yet come. So the Lord escaped from their hands and withdrew from them.

Now a leper came to him and said, 'Teacher Jesus, while I was travelling
with lepers and eating with them at the inn, I contracted leprosy myself. But
if you are willing, I can be made clean.'

The Lord said to him, 'I am willing: be clean.' And immediately the
leprosy departed from him.

Then Jesus said to him, 'Go and show yourself to the priests and make an
offering for the cleansing as Moses commanded and sin no more ...'

P.Egerton 2, fragment 2(→)

νομενοι πρὸς αὐτὸν ἐξ[ετασ-]
τικῶς ἐπείραζον αὐτὸν λ[έγοντες·]
διδάσκαλε Ἰη(σοῦ), οἴδαμεν ὅτι [ἀπὸ θ(εο)ῦ]
ἐλήλυθας· ἃ γὰρ ποιεῖς μα[ρτυρεῖ]
5 ὑπὲρ το[ὺ]ς προφ(ήτ)ας πάντας. [εἰπὲ οὖν]
ἡμῖν· ἐξὸν τοῖς βα(σι)λεῦσ[ιν ἀποδοῦ-]
ναι τὰ ἀγ[ή]κοντα τῇ ἀρχῇ; ἀπ[οδῶμεν αὐ-]
τοῖς ἢ μ[ή;] ὁ δὲ Ἰη(σοῦς) εἰδὼς [τὴν δι-]
άνοιαν [αὐτ]ῶν ἐμβριμ[ησάμενος]
10 εἶπεν α[ὐτοῖς]· τί με καλεῖτ[ε τῷ στό-]
ματι ὑμ[ῶν δι]δάσκαλον, ᾽μ[ὴ πράσσ-]
οντες᾽ ὃ [λ]έγω; καλῶς Ἡ[σ(αΐ)ας περὶ ὑ-]
μῶν ἐπ[ρο]φ(ήτευ)σεν εἰπῴν· ὁ [λαὸς οὖ-]
τος τοῖς [χείλ]εσιν αὐτ[ῶν τιμῶσιν]
15 με, ἡ [δὲ καρδί]α αὐτῷ[ν πόρρω ἀπέ-]
χει ἀπ᾽ ἐ[μοῦ· μ]άτῃ[ν με σέβονται,]
ἐντάλ[ματα

2(→) 1 ἐξεταστικῶς ἐπείραζον ... (4) ποιεῖς μαρτυρεῖ Bell-Skeat[1935a] ‖ 5 ὑπὲρ : ὕπερ pap. ‖ εἰπὲ οὖν Bell-Skeat[1935b] : λέγε οὖν Bell-Skeat[1935a] ‖ 6 ἡμῖν : ημειν pap. ‖ βασιλεῦσιν ἀποδοῦναι ... (11) ὑμῶν διδάσκαλον Bell-Skeat[1935a] ‖ 9 ἐμβριμ[ησάμενος] : εμβρειμ[ησαμενος] pap. ‖ 11 ὑμ[ῶν] : ὕμ[ων] pap. ‖ μὴ πράσσοντες Daniels[1990] : μὴ ἀκούοντες Bell-Skeat[1935a] ‖ 12 λέγω; καλῶς ... (16) σέβονται, ἐντάλματα Bell-Skeat[1935a]

... πρὸς αὐτὸν ἐξεταστικῶς ἐπείραζον αὐτὸν λέγοντες· διδάσκαλε Ἰησοῦ, οἴδαμεν ὅτι ἀπὸ θεοῦ ἐλήλυθας· ἃ γὰρ ποιεῖς μαρτυρεῖ ὑπὲρ τοὺς προφήτας πάντας. εἰπὲ οὖν ἡμῖν· ἐξὸν τοῖς βασιλεῦσιν ἀποδοῦναι τὰ ἀνήκοντα τῇ ἀρχῇ; ἀποδῶμεν αὐτοῖς ἢ μή; ὁ δὲ Ἰησοῦς εἰδὼς τὴν διάνοιαν αὐτῶν ἐμβριμησάμενος εἶπεν αὐτοῖς· τί με καλεῖτε τῷ στόματι ὑμῶν διδάσκαλον, μὴ πράσσοντες ὃ λέγω; καλῶς Ἡσαΐας περὶ ὑμῶν ἐπροφήτευσεν εἰπών· ὁ λαὸς οὗτος τοῖς χείλεσιν αὐτῶν τιμῶσιν με, ἡ δὲ καρδία αὐτῶν πόρρω ἀπέχει ἀπ᾽ ἐμοῦ· μάτην με σέβονται, ἐντάλματα ...

... to him, they tested him rigorously, saying, 'Teacher Jesus, we know that you have come from God. For the things that you are doing provide a testimony that is above and beyond all the prophets. So tell us: is it proper to pay kings the things that relate to their rule? Should we pay them or not?'

But since he knew their intention, Jesus scolded them and said, 'Why do you call me teacher with your mouths when you do not do what I say? Well did Isaiah prophesy about you when he said, "This people honours me with their lips, but their heart is far from me; in vain do they worship me ... commandments ..."'

P.Egerton 2, fragment 2(↓)

] τῷ τ[ό]πῳ [κα]τακλεισαν-
] ὑποτέτακ[τ]α̣[ι] ἀδήλως
] . . . τὸ̣ βάρο[ς α]ὐτοῦ ἄστα̣το(ν)
] ἀπο̣ρηθέντ̣ων δὲ ἐκεί-
5 [νων ὡς] πρὸς τὸ ξένον ἐπ[ε]ρώτημα
[αὐτοῦ π]εριπατῶν ὁ Ἰη(σοῦς) [ἐ]σ̣τάθη
[ἐπὶ τοῦ] χείλους τοῦ Ἰο[ρδά]νου
[ποταμ]οῦ καὶ ἐκτείνα[ς τὴν] χεῖ-
[ρα αὐτο]ῦ̣ τὴν δεξιὰν [. . .]μ̣ισεν
10   κ]αὶ κατέσπειρ[εν ἐπ]ὶ τὸν
]ον· καὶ τότε [. . .] κατε
]ενο̣γ ὕδωρ· ε . [. . .] . ν τ̣ὴν
]· καὶ επ . [. .]θη ενω
ἐ]ξήγα[γ]εν [. .] κ̣α̣ρπὸ(ν)
15   ]π̣ολλ[. . . . . .]εισχα
]τα[. . . . . . .]υτους·

2(↓) 2 ὑποτέτακ[τ]α̣[ι] : ῦποτετακ[τ]α̣[ι] pap. ‖ 4 ἐκείνων ὡς . . . (10) κατέσπειρεν ἐπὶ Bell-Skeat[1935a] ‖ 7 Ἰο[ρδά]νου : ϊο[ρδα]νου pap. ‖ 12 ὕδωρ : ϋδωρ pap.

... τῷ τόπῳ κατακλεισαν-(?) ... ὑποτέτακται ἀδήλως ... τὸ βάρος αὐτοῦ ἄστατον ... ἀπορηθέντων δὲ ἐκείνων ὡς πρὸς τὸ ξένον ἐπερώτημα αὐτοῦ περιπατῶν ὁ Ἰησοῦς ἐστάθη ἐπὶ τοῦ χείλους τοῦ Ἰορδάνου ποταμοῦ καὶ ἐκτείνας τὴν χεῖρα αὐτοῦ τὴν δεξιὰν ... καὶ κατέσπειρεν ἐπὶ τὸν ... καὶ τότε ... ὕδωρ ... τὴν ... καὶ ... ἐξήγαγεν ... καρπὸν ...

... being enclosed in the place ... placed underneath secretly ... its weight unweighed ... Then while they were perplexed as to his strange question, Jesus walked and stood on the bank of the Jordan river. And stretching out his right hand ... and he sowed on the ... and then ... water ... the ... and ... he brought forth ... fruit ...

P. Egerton 2, fragment 3 (↓)

```
    ] . παρη
    ]ς ἐὰν
    ] αὐτοῦ
    ]ημενος
5   ] εἰδὼς
    ]ηπ
```

P. Egerton 2, fragment 3 (→)

```
  ενεσα[
  μενωπ[
  ϛους εισ[
  κτεινω[
5 λέγει· ο[
  ]ε[
```

. . .
. . . if . . .
. . . of him/it
. . .
. . . knowing . . .
. . .

. . .
. . .
. . .
. . .
says . . .
. . .

OTHER UNIDENTIFIED GOSPEL FRAGMENTS

The six fascinating manuscripts included in this chapter were recovered from Egypt in the late nineteenth and early twentieth centuries. Both the 'Faiyum Fragment' (P.Vindob.G 2325) and the 'Fragment of an Uncanonical Gospel from Oxyrhynchus' (P.Oxy. 840) were published in multiple editions and discussed extensively at the time of their discovery, but interest was short-lived. The other four fragments (P.Mert. 51, P.Oxy. 210, P.Oxy. 1224 and P.Berol. 11710) never attracted the attention they deserved. All of these gospel fragments have been largely ignored for most of the past century, either having been buried anew in massive collections of 'New Testament Apocrypha' or simply set aside and forgotten.

Each of the manuscripts evidently preserves a portion of a different, unidentified gospel. The gospels recount teachings and activities of Jesus that are to be understood as having occurred during the time between his baptism and crucifixion.[1] P.Vindob.G 2325, P.Mert. 51, P.Oxy. 1224 and P.Berol. 11710 present alternative versions of episodes recorded in the New Testament gospels. P.Oxy. 840 includes an otherwise unattested story about Jesus visiting the temple with his disciples. The badly damaged text of P.Oxy. 210 preserves tantalizing excerpts apparently from a discourse of Jesus.

Although the different gospels preserved on these six manuscripts were undoubtedly cherished at one time by some of Jesus' followers, no traces of their use in antiquity have survived. There are no known allusions to any of them by ancient Christian writers, and the texts themselves do not provide the kind of internal clues that could be used to determine precisely when or where they were written. Were these long-lost gospels written early in the Christian movement or much later? Were they written before or after the New Testament gospels? Why were they written at all? Who might have valued them? What can they tell us about Jesus? The reader is free to decide.

---

1. The one possible exception is P.Oxy. 210, fragment 1(→), which might contain part of an infancy narrative. See S. E. Porter, 'POxy II 210 as an Apocryphal Gospel and the Development of Egyptian Christianity', in vol. 2 of *Atti del XXII Congresso internazionale di papirologia: Firenze, 23–29 agosto 1998* (eds. I. Andorlini, G. Bastianini, M. Manfredi and G. Menci; Firenze: Istituto papirologico 'G. Vitelli', 2001), pp. 1095–1108 (1101–02).

The Faiyum Fragment (P. Vindob. G 2325)

Contents: An account of Jesus predicting Peter's denial (cf. Mt. 26.30–35; Mk 14.26–31).

Date copied: Third century (Bickell).

Basic description: Papyrus roll(?); one fragment, w. 4.3 x h. 3.5 cm; 7 partially preserved lines of text.

Nomina sacra: πετ (Πέτρου).

Other notable features: Unusual nomina sacra πετ highlighted in red ink.

Current housing location: Österreichische Nationalbibliothek (Austrian National Library), Vienna.

Museum ID: G 2.325.

First published edition: G. Bickell, 'Ein Papyrusfragment eines nichtkanonischen Evangeliums', *ZKT* 9 (1885), pp. 498–504; 10 (1886), pp. 208–09.

Official publication + colour manuscript photo: G. Bickell, 'Das nichtkanonische Evangelienfragment', in vol. 1 of *Mittheilungen aus der Sammlung der Papyrus Erzherzog Rainer* (ed. J. Karabacek; Vienna: Verlag der k.k. Hofund Staatsdruckerei, 1887), pp. 53–61.

Critical edition: T. J. Kraus, 'P.Vindob.G 2325: Das sogenannte Fayûm-Evangelium – Neuedition und kritische Rückschlüsse', *ZAC* 5 (2001), pp. 197–212.

Merton Papyrus 51 (P. Mert. 51)

Contents: 1. A small fragment of a narrative in which the people and the tax collectors praise God, and the Pharisees (?) refuse to be baptized (cf. Lk. 7.29–30); 2. A saying about a tree, its fruit and the treasure of the heart (cf. Lk. 6.43–45; Mt. 7.17–20; 12.33–35).

Dated copied: Third century (Rees).

Basic description: Papyrus codex; part of one leaf, w. 3.9 x h. 5.3 cm; 16 partially preserved lines of text.

Nomina sacra: θυ (θεοῦ); θν (θεόν).

Other notable features: Initial letters enlarged in (↓).3–5 (i.e., all preserved initial letters enlarged); blank space apparently used to indicate conclusion of a paragraph or section; faint double point visible at the end of (→).7.

Current housing location: Chester Beatty Library, Dublin Castle.

Museum ID: Dublin, CBL MP 51.

First published edition (official publication) + colour manuscript photos: B. R. Rees, '51.Christian Fragment', in vol. 2 of *A Descriptive Catalogue of the Greek Papyri in the Collection of Wilfred Merton, F.S.A.* (eds. B. R. Rees, H. I. Bell and J. W. B. Barns; Dublin: Hodges Figgis & Co., 1959), pp. 1–4.

Oxyrhynchus Papyrus 210 (P.Oxy. 210)

Contents: 1. An extremely damaged narrative that mentions an angel (perhaps cf. Mt. 1.24); 2. An apparent discourse of Jesus in which he speaks about a good tree bringing forth good fruit (cf. Lk. 6.43–45; Mt. 7.17–20; 12.33–35) and apparently declares that 'I am' the image of God (cf. 2 Cor. 4.4; Col. 1.15) and in the form of God (cf. Phil. 2.6).

Date copied: Third century (Grenfell and Hunt).

Basic description: Papyrus codex; two fragments (possibly from one leaf), w. 8.7 x h. 17.3 cm (fragment 1), tiny (fragment 2); 45 partially preserved lines of text.

Nomina sacra: Probably α̅ν̅ο̅ς̅ (ἄνθρωπος); θ̅ς̅ (θεός); θ̅υ̅ (θεοῦ); θ̅ω̅ (θεῷ); probably ι̅η̅ς̅ (Ἰησοῦς); π̅ρ̅ς̅ (πατρός).

Other notable features: Apostrophe appears occasionally between consonants.

Current housing location: University Library, University of Cambridge.

Museum ID: Add. Ms. 4048.

First published edition (official publication): B. P. Grenfell and A. S. Hunt, '210. Early Christian Fragment', in vol. 2 of *The Oxyrhynchus Papyri* (London: Egypt Exploration Fund, 1899), pp. 9–10.

Critical edition: S. E. Porter, 'POxy II 210 as an Apocryphal Gospel and the Development of Egyptian Christianity', in vol. 2 of *Atti del XXII Congresso internazionale di papirologia: Firenze, 23–29 agosto 1998* (eds. I. Andorlini, G. Bastianini, M. Manfredi and G. Menci; Firenze: Istituto papirologico 'G. Vitelli', 2001), pp. 1095–1108.

Other important published edition: C. H. Roberts, 'An Early Christian Papyrus', in *Miscellània papirològica Ramon Roca-Puig* (ed. S. Janeras; Barcelona: Fundació Salvador Vives Casajuana, 1987), pp. 293–96.

Oxyrhynchus Papyrus 1224 (P.Oxy. 1224)

Contents: 1. An apparently first-person account of someone's vision of Jesus; 2. A dispute about a new teaching (cf. Mk 1.27); 3. Jesus' reply to the criticism that he associates with sinners (cf. Lk. 5.27–32; Mt. 9.9–13; Mk 2.13–17); 4. A discourse including the injunction to pray for one's enemies (cf. *Did.* 1.3; Mt. 5.44; Lk. 6.27) and a statement about who is really for and against you (cf. Lk. 9.50).

Date copied: Late third or early fourth century (Grenfell and Hunt).

Basic description: Papyrus codex; two fragments, w. 4.6 x h. 4.0 cm (fragment 1), w. 13.1 x h. 6.3 cm (fragment 2); 28 partially preserved lines of text.

Nomina sacra: ι̅η̅ (Ἰησοῦς, Ἰησοῦ).

Other notable features: Unclear whether fragments 1 and 2 contain different parts of same text or different texts; fragment 1(→) labelled page ρλθ (139); page number lost from fragment 1(↓); four columns of fragment 2 (two on each side) evidently four single-column pages; fragment 2(→), column ii presumably labelled ρογ (173); fragment 2(↓), column i labelled page ροδ (174); fragment 2(↓), column ii presumably labelled ροε (175); fragment 2(→), column i apparently labelled page ρος (176); some final nus suppressed, indicated by a supralinear stroke over the preceding letter.

Current housing location: Bodleian Library, University of Oxford.

Museum ID: MS. Gr. Th. e. 8 (P).

First published edition (official publication) + colour photos of fragments 1(→) and 2(↓): B. P. Grenfell and A. S. Hunt, '1224. Uncanonical Gospel', in vol. 10 of *The Oxyrhynchus Papyri* (London: Egypt Exploration Fund, 1914), pp. 1–10.

Oxyrhynchus Parchment 840 (P.Oxy. 840)

Contents: A narrative in which Jesus goes into the temple with his disciples and has a dispute with a Pharisee about what it means to be truly 'clean' (cf. Mt. 23.25–26; Lk. 11.39–40).

Date copied: Fourth century (Grenfell and Hunt).

Basic description: Parchment (vellum) codex; most of one leaf, w. 7.4 x h. 8.8 cm; 45 mostly preserved lines of text.

Nomina sacra: ανων (ἀνθρώπων); δδ (Δαυίδ); σωρ (σωτήρ); σωρι (σωτῆρι).

Other notable features: Handwriting of miniature codex practically microscopic but still readable; frequent punctuation in the form of the middle point; longer pauses marked not only by dots but also short blank spaces and enlarged letters; one circumflex, one acute accent visible; red ink used to highlight punctuation, initial letters of sentences, strokes of abbreviation and accents; some final nus suppressed, indicated by a supralinear stroke over the preceding letter.

Current housing location: Bodleian Library, University of Oxford.

Museum ID: MS. Gr. Th. g. 11.

First published edition: B. P. Grenfell and A. S. Hunt, *Fragment of an Uncanonical Gospel from Oxyrhynchus* (London: Oxford University Press, 1908).

Official publication + colour photo of manuscript front: B. P. Grenfell and A. S. Hunt, '840. Fragment of an Uncanonical Gospel', in vol. 5 of *The Oxyrhynchus Papyri* (London: Egypt Exploration Fund, 1908), pp. 1–10.

Critical edition: M. J. Kruger, *The Gospel of the Savior: An Analysis of P. Oxy. 840 and its Place in the Gospel Traditions of Early Christianity* (eds. S. E. Porter and W. J. Porter; Texts and Editions for New Testament Study, 1; Leiden: Brill, 2005).

Berlin Papyrus 11710 (P.Berol. 11710)

Contents: An exchange between Jesus and Nathanael (cf. Jn 1.49; 1.29).

Date copied: Sixth century (Schubart/Lietzmann).

Basic description: Papyrus codex; two well-preserved leaves, approximately w. 6.5 x h. 7.5 cm each; 23 complete lines (21 Greek + 2 Coptic).

Nomina sacra: θ̅υ̅ (θεοῦ); ι̅ς̅ (Ἰησοῦς); κ̅ε̅ (κύριε); χ̅ς̅ (χριστός).

Other notable features: Back page of codex decorated with Coptic letters and symbols (Ɽ, ⳨).

Current housing location: Ägyptisches Museum und Papyrussammlung (Egyptian Museum and Papyrus Collection), Berlin.

Museum ID: P 11710.

First published edition: H. Lietzmann, 'Ein apokryphes Evangelien-fragment', *ZNW* 22 (1923), pp. 153–54.

The Faiyum Fragment

P. Vindob. G 2325

[ἐν δὲ τῷ ἐ]ξάγειν ὡς ε̣[ἶ]πε̣[ν] ὅ̣τι ἅ[παντες]
[ἐν ταύτῃ] τῇ νυκτὶ σκανδαλισ[θήσεσ-]
[θε κατὰ] τὸ γραφέν· πατάξω τὸν [ποιμέ-]
[να καὶ τὰ] πρόβατα διασκορπισθήσ[εται. εἰ-]
5　[πόντος 'το]ῦ̣' Πέτ(ρου)· καὶ εἰ πάντες, ο[ὐκ ἐγώ.]
[λέγει Ἰ(ησοῦ)ς· πρὶ]ν ἀλεκτρυὼν δὶς κοκ[κύσει,]
　　　τρὶς ἀ]π̣α̣ρ̣γ̣[ήσῃ με

---

1 ἐν δὲ ... ὅτι ἅπαντες Wessely[1906] ‖ 2 ἐν ταύτῃ ... (4) καὶ τὰ Bickell[1885] ‖ 4 διασκορπισθήσεται Hilgenfeld[1886] : διασκορπισθήσονται Bickell[1885] ‖ εἰπόντος Bickell[1885] ‖ 5 τοῦ Bickell[1885] : ἐμοῦ Lührmann[1993] ‖ Πέτ(ρου) : π̇ε̇τ̇ (coloured over in red ink) pap. ‖ οὐκ ἐγώ Bickell[1885] ‖ 6 [λέγει Ἰ(ησοῦ)ς· πρὶ]ν ἀλεκτρυὼν δὶς κοκ[κύσει] Wessely[1906] : [ὁ κ(ύριο)ς· πρὶν ἢ] ὁ ἀλεκτρυὼν δὶς κοκ[κύσει] Usener[1889] : [ἔφη αὐτῷ·] ὁ ἀλεκτρυὼν δὶς κοκ[κύξει] Bickell[1885] ‖ 7 τρὶς ἀπαρνήσῃ με Bickell[1885]

... ἐν δὲ τῷ ἐξάγειν ὡς εἶπεν ὅτι ἄπαντες ἐν ταύτῃ τῇ νυκτὶ σκανδαλισθήσεσθε κατὰ τὸ γραφέν· πατάξω τὸν ποιμένα καὶ τὰ πρόβατα διασκορπισθήσεται. εἰπόντος τοῦ Πέτρου· καὶ εἰ πάντες, οὐκ ἐγώ. λέγει Ἰησοῦς· πρὶν ἀλεκτρυὼν δὶς κοκκύσει ... τρὶς ἀπαρνήσῃ με ...

... as he brought them out, he said, 'You will all fall away this night as it is written, "I will strike the shepherd and the sheep will be scattered."'

Peter said, 'Even if all do so, I will not.'

Jesus said, 'Before the rooster crows twice, you will deny me three times ...'

Merton Papyrus 51

P. Mert. 51 (→)

πᾶς ὁ λα]ὸς καὶ οἱ τελῶ[ναι]
[ἀκούσαντες ἐδικ]αίωσαν τὸν θ(εὸ)ν
[ὁμολογοῦντες τὰς] ἁμαρτίας ἑαυτῶν.
[οἱ δὲ Φαρισαῖοι ο]ὐκ ἐβαπτίσαντο
5   βουλ]ὴν τοῦ θ(εο)ῦ
        θ(εο)]ῦ ἠθέτησαν
     ] ἀθετεῖ :
     μ]ετ᾿ αὐτο[ῦ]

P. Mert. 51 (↓)

[πονη]ροῦ προφερ[. . . . . προ-]
[ἐ]φερεν ὡς ἐκ π[ονηροῦ . . . . . δένδ-]
ρον καὶ ὅτε ἀποσ[τέλλετε ἐκ τοῦ ἀγα-]
θοῦ θησαυροῦ τῆ[ς καρδίας
5 ἀπόλλυτ[αι
    ]τησουκαρ[
    ] οὐ ποιεῖτε [
     ]ουλε . [

(→) 1 πᾶς ὁ . . . (4) Φαρισαῖοι οὐκ Rees[1959] ‖ 5 βουλὴν Rees[1959] ‖ 6 θεοῦ Rees[1959] ‖ 8 μετ᾿ αὐτοῦ Rees[1959]
(↓) 1 πονηροῦ Rees[1959] ‖ προέφερεν Rees[1959] ‖ 2 πονηροῦ Rees[1959] ‖ δένδρον καὶ . . . (4) τῆς καρδίας Rees[1959] ‖ 4 θησαυροῦ : θηουρου pap.

... πᾶς ὁ λαὸς καὶ οἱ τελῶναι ἀκούσαντες ἐδικαίωσαν τὸν θεὸν ὁμολογοῦντες τὰς ἁμαρτίας ἑαυτῶν. οἱ δὲ Φαρισαῖοι οὐκ ἐβαπτίσαντο ... βουλὴν τοῦ θεοῦ ... θεοῦ ἠθέτησαν ... ἀθετεῖ ... μετ᾽ αὐτοῦ ...

... the whole people and the tax collectors heard and declared God just, confessing their sins. But the Pharisees were not baptized ... purpose of God ... of God they rejected ... rejects ... with him ...

... πονηροῦ προφερ-(?) ... προέφερεν ὡς ἐκ πονηροῦ ... δένδρον καὶ ὅτε ἀποστέλλετε ἐκ τοῦ ἀγαθοῦ θησαυροῦ τῆς καρδίας ... ἀπόλλυται ... οὐ ποιεῖτε ...

... of bad producing ... produced as from bad ... tree and when you send out from the good treasure of the heart ... destroy ... not do ...

Oxyrhynchus Papyrus 210

P.Oxy. 210, fragment 1 (→)

```
      ]αρτη[ . . . ]αλ[
      ]εξει ι[ . . . ]ναγ[
      ]ρσιν οὐ δύνατα[ι
      ὑ]πομεῖναι δὲ πο[
 5    ἔ]ταξε ἄγγελος πα[
      πε]ρὶ ἀγγέλου λεχ[
      . . . ς ἡμῖν τὰ α[
      ναται ου[
      οὗτος τα[
10    ἔτι εξ . [ . ] α
      τιαπ[
      δου[
      οπε[
      [
15    [
      [
      σει . . .
```

1(→) 2 εξει ι : εξει ϊ pap. ‖ 6 ἀγγέλου : αγ᾿γελου pap. ‖ 7 ἡμῖν : ημειν pap.

. . .

. . .

. . . cannot . . .

. . . to endure but . . .

. . . angel ordered . . .

. . . about an angel . . .

. . . to us the . . .

. . .

this . . .

still . . .

. . .

. . .

. . .

. . .

. . .

. . .

. . .

P.Oxy. 210, fragment 1(↓)

```
            ]μ[
            ]γ[
            .[ . ]πελ[
            ] ἀγαθο[-
   5        ] ἔλεγε ạ[
            ] ι̣ π(ατ)ρ(ὸ)ς υ[
            ]ν ἀγα[θο-
            ]το[
            ] . . ρο̣ι[
   10       ἀγα]θὸν το[
            ] ἐνεγκο̣[-
        ] θ(εὸ)ς ὁ [ . . . ] ἀλλὰ [
        ]α Ἰη[(σοῦ)ς κα]ὶ ἐρεῖ τ[
       ἀγα]θοὺς [ἐν]έγκει ὁ [θ(εὸ)ς
   15   ἐ]νέγ[κει ἀ]γαθὸς [
       καρ]π̣ὸς δ[ἐν]δρου ἀγαθοῦ
          ] ὑπὸ [τὸ ἀ]γαθὸν ἐγώ εἰμι
           ]τ̣ο εἰμι εἰκὼν τῆς [
          ] ὃ̣ς ἐν μορφῇ θ(εο)ῦ
   20     ]δια ὡς εἰκὼν αυ
```

1(↓) 6 υ[: ϋ[pap. ‖ 11 ἐνεγκο̣[: ενεγ'κο̣[pap. ‖ 13 Ἰη[(σοῦ)ς κα]ὶ Porter[2001] : ιη[. κα]ὶ Grenfell-Hunt[1899] ‖ 14 ἀγαθοὺς Grenfell-Hunt[1899] ‖ [ἐν]έγκει Grenfell-Hunt[1899] : [εν]εγ'κει pap. ‖ ὁ [θ(εὸ)ς Porter[2001] : o[θ̅ς̅] pap. ‖ 15 [ἐ]νέγ[κει ἀ]γαθὸς Porter[2001] : [ἐ]νέγ[κ . ἀ]γαθὸς Grenfell-Hunt[1899] ‖ 16 καρπὸς δένδρου Grenfell-Hunt[1899] ‖ 17 [τὸ ἀ]γαθὸν Porter[2001] : [. . ἀ]γαθὸν Grenfell-Hunt[1899]

. . .

. . .

. . .

. . . good . . .

. . . he said . . .

. . . father . . .

. . . good . . .

. . .

. . .

. . . good . . .

. . . bear . . .

. . . God who . . . but . . .

. . . Jesus and he will say . . .

. . . good. God bears . . .

. . . a good bears . . .

. . . fruit of a good tree . . .

. . . under the good. I am . . .

. . . I am the image of the . . .

. . . who in the form of God

. . . as the image . . .

] . θ(ε)ῷ θ(ε)ῷ τῷ
]ν τοῦ εἶναι
]ειται ὁρατὰ
]ντα τοῦ αι̣[
25   ] ιδεν ὅτι [
]ε̣αν ιδεν[
]νοσεπ[
] ἄν(θρωπ)ο̣ς π . [

P. Oxy. 210, fragment 2

]λλ[
2]ν̣η̣ι̣[

25 ιδεν : ϊδεν pap. ‖ 26 ιδεν : ϊδεν pap.

. . . to God, to God, who
. . . of the being
. . . visible things
. . . of the . . .
. . . that . . .

. . .

. . .

. . . human being . . .

Oxyrhynchus Papyrus 1224

P.Oxy. 1224, page 139

]γτι ἐν παντὶ
] . ων. ἀμὴν ὑ-
3 [μῖν λέγω . . . .]εισ[

P.Oxy. 1224, page 140(?)

σεται ὑμεῖς [
2   ] . ητ[

P.Oxy. 1224, page 173

με ἐβάρησεν. καὶ [
μου Ἰη(σοῦ) [ἐ]γ ὀράμα[τι
τιαθ[. .]εις οὐ γὰρ [
]υ ἀλλὰ ο[
5 δουσεπ[

139 2 ὑ[μῖν] : ὕ[μιν] pap. ‖ ὑμῖν λέγω Grenfell-Hunt[1914]
140 1 ὑμεῖς : ὕμεις pap.
173 2 ἐν ὀράματι Grenfell-Hunt[1914]

. . . in everything
. . . Truly,
I say to you . . .

. . . you . . .
. . .

. . . με ἐβάρησεν. καὶ . . . Ἰησοῦ ἐν ὁράματι . . . οὐ γὰρ . . . ἀλλὰ . . .

. . . weighed me down. And . . . Jesus in a vision . . . for not . . . but . . .

P.Oxy. 1224, page 174

```
      ]πες μὴ ἀποκρινό-
[μενος . . . ἀ]πεῖπας. π[ο]ίαν σέ
[φασιν διδα]χὴν καιν[ὴν] δι-
[δάσκειν; . . . ] . [ . . . . ]α καινὸ(ν)
5                    ]θητι καὶ
```

P.Oxy. 1224, page 175

```
οἱ δὲ γραμματεῖς κα[ὶ Φαρισαῖ-]
οι καὶ ἱερεῖς θεασάμ[ενοι αὐ-]
τὸν ἠγανάκτουν [ὅτι σὺν ἁμαρ-]
τωλοῖς ἀνὰ μέ[σον κεῖται. ὁ]
5  δὲ Ἰη(σοῦς) ἀκούσας [εἶπεν· οὐ χρείαν]
[ἔχ]ουσιν οἱ ὑ[γιαίνοντες ἰατ-]
[ροῦ.
```

174 1 ἀποκρινό[μενος] Grenfell-Hunt[1914] : αποκρεινο[μενος] pap. ‖ 2 ἀπεῖπας. ποίαν . . .
(3) καινὴν διδάσκειν Grenfell-Hunt[1914]
175 1 καὶ Φαρισαῖοι . . . (6) ὑγιαίνοντες ἰατροῦ Grenfell-Hunt[1914] ‖ 2 ἱερεῖς : ἱερεις pap. ‖
6 ὑ[γιαίνοντες] : ὑ[γιανοντες] pap.

... μὴ ἀποκρινόμενος ... ἀπεῖπας. ποίαν σέ φασιν διδαχὴν καινὴν διδάσκειν; ... καινὸν ... καὶ ...

... not answering ... you renounced ... What is the new teaching that they say you teach? ... new ... and ...

... οἱ δὲ γραμματεῖς καὶ Φαρισαῖοι καὶ ἱερεῖς θεασάμενοι αὐτὸν ἠγανάκτουν ὅτι σὺν ἁμαρτωλοῖς ἀνὰ μέσον κεῖται. ὁ δὲ Ἰησοῦς ἀκούσας εἶπεν· οὐ χρείαν ἔχουσιν οἱ ὑγιαίνοντες ἰατροῦ ...

... Now when the scribes, Pharisees and priests saw him, they were angry that he was reclining in the midst of sinners.

But when Jesus heard, he said, 'Those who are healthy have no need of a physician ...'

P.Oxy. 1224, page 176

κ]αὶ π[ρ]οσεύχεσθε ὑπὲρ
[τῶν ἐχθ]ρῶν ὑμῶν· ὁ γὰρ μὴ ὢ(ν)
[κατὰ ὑμ]ῶν ὑπὲρ ὑμῶν ἐστιν.
    ]ν μακρὰν αὔριον
5   γ]ενήσεται καὶ ἐν
    ] τοῦ ἀντιδί[κου]
    ] ινενωγ[

176 1 καὶ προσεύχεσθε . . . (3) κατὰ ὑμῶν Grenfell-Hunt[1914] ‖ ὑπὲρ : ὕπερ pap. ‖ 2 ὑμῶν : ὕμων pap. ‖ 3 ὑπὲρ : ὕπερ pap. ‖ ὑμῶν : ὕμων pap. ‖ 6 ἀντιδίκου Grenfell-Hunt[1914]

. . . καὶ προσεύχεσθε ὑπὲρ τῶν ἐχθρῶν ὑμῶν· ὁ γὰρ μὴ ὢν κατὰ ὑμῶν ὑπὲρ ὑμῶν ἐστιν . . . μακρὰν αὔριον . . . γενήσεται καὶ ἐν . . . τοῦ ἀντιδίκου . . .

'. . . and pray for your enemies. For the one who is not against you is for you . . . far away tomorrow . . . will be and in . . . the adversary . . .'

Oxyrhynchus Parchment 840

P.Oxy. 840, front

πρότερον προαδικῆσαι πάντα σοφίζεται. ἀλλὰ προσέχετε μή πως καὶ
ὑμεῖς τὰ ὅμοια αὐτοῖς πάθητε· οὐ γὰρ
ἐν τοῖς ʽζωοῖςʼ μόνοις ἀπολαμβάνου-
5 σιν οἱ κακοῦργοι τῶν ἀν(θρώπ)ων ἀλλὰ [κ]αὶ
κόλασιν ʽὑπομενοῦσινʼ καὶ πολ[λ]ὴν
βάσανον. καὶ παραλαβὼν αὐτοὺς
εἰσήγαγεν εἰς αὐτὸ τὸ ἁγνευτήριον κ̣αὶ
περιεπάτει ἐν τῷ ἱερῷ. καὶ προσε[λ-]
10 θὼν Φαρισαῖός τις ἀρχιερεὺς . . . [
τὸ ὄνομα συνέτυχεν αὐτοῖς καὶ ε[ἶπεν]
τῷ σω(τῆ)ρι· τίς ἐπέτρεψέν σοι πατ[εῖν]
τοῦτο τὸ ἁγνευτήριον καὶ ἰδεῖν [ταῦ-]
τα τὰ ἅγια σκεύη μή̀τεʹ λουσα[μ]έν[ῳ] μ̣[ή-]
15 τε ʽμὴνʹ τῶν μαθητῶν σου τοὺς π[όδας βα-]
πτισθέντων; ἀλλὰ μεμολυ[μμένος]
ἐπάτησας τοῦτο τὸ ἱερόν, τ[όπον ὄν-]
τα καθαρόν, ὃν οὐδεὶς ἄ[λλος εἰ μὴ]

---

front 3 ὑμεῖς : ὕμεις ms. ‖ 4 ζωοῖς : ζῴοις ‖ 6 ὑπομενοῦσιν : ὑπομένουσιν : ὑπομενουσιν ms. ‖
11 εἶπεν τῷ . . . (18) εἰ μὴ Grenfell-Hunt[1908a] ‖ 13 ἰδεῖν : ἴδειν ms. ‖ 17 ἱερόν : ἱερον ms.

πρότερον προαδικῆσαι πάντα σοφίζεται. ἀλλὰ προσέχετε μή πως καὶ
ὑμεῖς τὰ ὅμοια αὐτοῖς πάθητε· οὐ γὰρ ἐν τοῖς ζωοῖς μόνοις
ἀπολαμβάνουσιν οἱ κακοῦργοι τῶν ἀνθρώπων ἀλλὰ καὶ κόλασιν
ὑπομενοῦσιν καὶ πολλὴν βάσανον. καὶ παραλαβὼν αὐτοὺς εἰσήγαγεν εἰς
αὐτὸ τὸ ἁγνευτήριον καὶ περιεπάτει ἐν τῷ ἱερῷ. καὶ προσελθὼν
Φαρισαῖός τις ἀρχιερεὺς . . . τὸ ὄνομα συνέτυχεν αὐτοῖς καὶ εἶπεν τῷ
σωτῆρι· τίς ἐπέτρεψέν σοι πατεῖν τοῦτο τὸ ἁγνευτήριον καὶ ἰδεῖν ταῦτα
τὰ ἅγια σκεύη μήτε λουσαμένῳ μήτε μὴν τῶν μαθητῶν σου τοὺς πόδας
βαπτισθέντων; ἀλλὰ μεμολυμμένος ἐπάτησας τοῦτο τὸ ἱερόν, τόπον ὄντα
καθαρόν, ὃν οὐδεὶς ἄλλος εἰ μὴ

' . . . earlier, before doing wrong, he reasons everything out slyly. You,
however, be careful that you do not also suffer the same kinds of things
as they do. For humanity's criminals not only receive retribution among
the living, but they will also endure punishment and much torture in the
future.'

Then he took them along, brought them into the place of purification
itself, and walked around in the temple. A certain Pharisee, a high priest
whose name was . . . , came to meet them and said to the saviour, 'Who
allowed you to set foot in this place of purification and to view these holy
vessels, when you have not bathed and your disciples have not even washed
their feet? Although you are unclean, you have set foot in this temple, a
place that is clean. Nobody

λουσάμενος καὶ ἀλλά[ξας τὰ ἐνδύ-]
20 ματα πατεῖ, οὐδὲ ὁ[ρᾶν τολμᾷ ταῦτα]
τὰ ἅγια σκεύη. καὶ σ[ταθεὶς ὁ σω(τὴ)ρ]
σ[ὺν τ]οῖς μαθηταῖ[ς ἀπεκρίθη αὐτῷ·]

P. Oxy. 840, back

σὺ οὖγ ἐνταῦθα ὢν ἐν τῷ ἱερῷ καθαρεύεις; λέγει αὐτῷ ʼἐκεῖνοςʻ· καθαρεύω· ἐλουσά-
25 μην γὰρ ἐν τῇ λίμνῃ τοῦ Δ(αυί)δ· καὶ δι' ἑτέρας κλίμακος κατελθὼν δι' ἑτέρας
ἀ[ν]ῆλθον, καὶ λευκὰ ἐνδύματα ἐνεδυσάμην καὶ καθαρά, καὶ τότε ἦλθο(ν)
καὶ προσέβλεψα τούτοις τοῖς ἁγίοις
30 σκεύεσιν. ὁ σω(τὴ)ρ πρὸς αὐτὸν ἀπο-
[κρι]θεὶς εἶπεν· οὐαί, τυφλοὶ μὴ ὁρῶ(ν)-
τ[ε]ς· σὺ ἐλούσω τούτοις τοῖς χεομένοις
ὕ[δ]ασι<ν>, ἐν οἷς κύνες καὶ χοῖροι βέβλην-
[ται] νυκτὸς καὶ ἡμέρας· καὶ νιψάμε-
35 [ν]ος τὸ ἐκτὸς δέρμα ἐσμήξω, ὅπερ

---

19 ἀλλάξας τὰ... (20) τολμᾷ ταῦτα Grenfell-Hunt[1908a] ‖ 21 σταθεὶς Bernhard : σταθεὶς εὐθὺς Swete[1908] : στὰς εὐθέως Grenfell-Hunt[1908a] ‖ ὁ σωτήρ... (22) ἀπεκρίθη αὐτῷ Grenfell-Hunt[1908a]

back 23 ὢν : ὂν ms. ‖ ἱερῷ : ἴερω ms. ‖ 26 κλίμακος : κλειμακος ms. ‖ 30 ἀποκριθεὶς εἶπεν... (34) καὶ νιψάμενος Grenfell-Hunt[1908a]

λουσάμενος καὶ ἀλλάξας τὰ ἐνδύματα πατεῖ, οὐδὲ ὁρᾶν τολμᾷ ταῦτα τὰ
ἅγια σκεύη. καὶ σταθεὶς ὁ σωτὴρ σὺν τοῖς μαθηταῖς ἀπεκρίθη αὐτῷ· σὺ
οὖν ἐνταῦθα ὢν ἐν τῷ ἱερῷ καθαρεύεις; λέγει αὐτῷ ἐκεῖνος· καθαρεύω·
ἐλουσάμην γὰρ ἐν τῇ λίμνῃ τοῦ Δαυίδ· καὶ δι' ἑτέρας κλίμακος κατελθὼν
δι' ἑτέρας ἀνῆλθον, καὶ λευκὰ ἐνδύματα ἐνεδυσάμην καὶ καθαρά, καὶ τότε
ἦλθον καὶ προσέβλεψα τούτοις τοῖς ἁγίοις σκεύεσιν. ὁ σωτὴρ πρὸς
αὐτὸν ἀποκριθεὶς εἶπεν· οὐαί, τυφλοὶ μὴ ὁρῶντες· σὺ ἐλούσω τούτοις
τοῖς χεομένοις ὕδασιν, ἐν οἷς κύνες καὶ χοῖροι βέβληνται νυκτὸς καὶ
ἡμέρας· καὶ νιψάμενος τὸ ἐκτὸς δέρμα ἐσμήξω, ὅπερ

sets foot in it or dares to view these holy vessels unless he has bathed and
changed his clothes beforehand.'

The saviour stood with his disciples and answered him, 'Since you are
here in the temple, are you clean?'

The Pharisee† said to the saviour‡, 'I am clean. For I bathed in the pool
of David. I went down into it by one staircase and came up out of it by
another. Then I put on white, clean clothes. And only then did I come and
look upon these holy vessels.'

The saviour answered him, 'How terrible it is for blind people who do
not see! You have bathed in the very same gushing waters where dogs and
pigs lie night and day. And you have washed and cleansed the outer layer
of skin –

† lit. 'he'
‡ lit. 'him'

[κα]ὶ αἱ πόρναι καὶ α[ἱ] αὐλητρίδες μυρί-
[ζ]ου[σιν κ]αὶ λούουσιν καὶ σμήχουσι
[καὶ κ]αλλωπίζουσι πρὸς ἐπιθυμί-
[αν τ]ῶν ἀν(θρώπ)ων, ἔνδοθεν δὲ ἐκεῖ-
40 [ναι πεπλ]ήρω<ν>ται σκορπίων καὶ
[πάσης κα]κίας. ἐγὼ δὲ καὶ οἱ
[μαθηταί μου] οὓς λέγεις μὴ βεβα-
[πτίσθαι βεβά]μμεθα ἐν ὕδασι ζω
           ]ς ἐλθοῦσι<ν> ἀπὸ . .
45   ἀλ]λὰ οὐαὶ [τ]οῖς [

36 καὶ αἱ . . . (42) βεβαπτίσθαι βεβάμμεθα Grenfell-Hunt[1908a] ‖ αὐλητρίδες : αυλητρίδες ms. ‖
43 ὕδασι : ὐδασι ms. ‖ 45 ἀλλὰ οὐαὶ τοῖς Grenfell-Hunt[1908a]

καὶ αἱ πόρναι καὶ αἱ αὐλητρίδες μυρίζουσιν καὶ λούουσιν καὶ σμήχουσι καὶ καλλωπίζουσι πρὸς ἐπιθυμίαν τῶν ἀνθρώπων, ἔνδοθεν δὲ ἐκεῖναι πεπλήρωνται σκορπίων καὶ πάσης κακίας. ἐγὼ δὲ καὶ οἱ μαθηταί μου οὓς λέγεις μὴ βεβαπτίσθαι βεβάμμεθα ἐν ὕδασι . . . ἐλθοῦσιν . . . ἀλλὰ οὐαὶ τοῖς . . .

this is the layer that prostitutes and flute-girls anoint, bathe, cleanse and adorn to arouse the lust of men, even though they are filled with scorpions and every kind of wickedness on the inside. But my disciples and I, whom you say have not washed, we have dipped in waters . . . come from . . . but how terrible it is for those who . . .'

Berlin Papyrus 11710

P. Berol. 11710, fragment a(↓)

θ . ιεσον καὶ
εἶπε· ῥαββιο-
ύ, κ(ύρι)ε, σὺ εἶ ὁ υἱ-
ὸς τοῦ θεοῦ. <ἀπεκρίθη αὐτῷ>
5 ὁ ῥαββὶς καὶ
εἶπε· Ναθα-
ναήλ,

P. Berol. 11710, fragment a(→)

πορεύου ἐν τ-
ῷ ἡλίῳ. ἀπεκ-
10 ρίθη αὐτῷ Να-
θαναὴλ καὶ
εἶπεν· ῥαβ-
βιού, κ(ύρι)ε, σὺ εἶ
ὁ ἀμνὸς

P. Berol. 11710, fragment b(↓)

15 τοῦ θ(εο)ῦ ὁ αἴρ-
ων τὰς ἁμ<α>-
ρ<τί>α<ς> τοῦ κόσ-
μο<υ>. ἀπεκρ-
ίθη αὐτῷ ὁ ῥ-
20 αββὶς καὶ
εἶπεν . .

P. Berol. 11710, fragment b(→)

℞ Ι(ΗϹΟΥ)Ϲ Χ(ΡΙϹΤΟ)Ϲ ΠΝΟ-
23 ΥΤΕ {Π}

θ✝

---

a(↓) 2 ῥαββιού : ραμβιου pap. ‖ 3 υἱὸς : ϋϊος pap. ‖ 5 ῥαββὶς : ραμβις pap. ‖ 6 Ναθαναήλ : ναθαναηλα pap.
a(→) 9 ἡλίῳ : ηλιο pap. ‖ ἀπεκρίθη : απεκριθι pap. ‖ 12 ῥαββιού : ραμβιου pap.
b(↓) 15 αἴρων : ερον pap. ‖ 18 ἀπεκρίθη : απεκριθι pap. ‖ 19 ῥαββὶς : ραμβις pap.
b(→) Despite the language switch from Greek to Coptic, there is no change in script (or scribe).

. . . καὶ εἶπε· ῥαββιού, κύριε, σὺ εἶ ὁ υἱὸς τοῦ θεοῦ. ἀπεκρίθη αὐτῷ ὁ ῥαββὶς καὶ εἶπε· Ναθαναήλ, πορεύου ἐν τῷ ἡλίῳ. ἀπεκρίθη αὐτῷ Ναθαναὴλ καὶ εἶπεν· ῥαββιού, κύριε, σὺ εἶ ὁ ἀμνὸς τοῦ θεοῦ ὁ αἴρων τὰς ἁμαρτίας τοῦ κόσμου. ἀπεκρίθη αὐτῷ ὁ ῥαββὶς καὶ εἶπεν . . .

ⲒⲎⲤⲞⲨⲤ ⲬⲢⲒⲤⲦⲞⲤ ⲠⲚⲞⲨⲦⲈ

. . . and he said, 'Rabbi, Lord, you are the son of God.'

The rabbi answered him and said, 'Nathanael, walk in the sun.'

Nathanael answered him and said, 'Rabbi, Lord, you are the lamb of God, who takes away the sins of the world.'

The rabbi answered him and said . . .

Jesus Christ God

BIBLIOGRAPHY

Akagi, T., 'The Literary Development of the Coptic Gospel of Thomas' (unpublished doctoral dissertation; Western Reserve University, 1965).

Aland, K., *Repertorium der griechischen christlichen Papyri I: Biblische Papyri* (Patristische Texte und Studien, 18; Berlin: Walter de Gruyter, 1976).

—— B. Aland, J. Karavidopoulos, C. M. Martini and B. M. Metzger (eds.), *Novum Testamentum Graece* (Stuttgart: Deutsche Bibelgesellschaft, 27th rev. edn, 1993).

—— *Synopsis Quattuor Evangeliorum* (Stuttgart: Deutsche Bibelgesellschaft, 15th edn, 1997).

Allen, W. C., 'The "New Sayings of Jesus"', *Guardian* (London: July 27, 1904), pp. 1254–55.

Attridge, H. W., 'The Original Text of Gos. Thom., Saying 30', *BASP* 16 (1979), pp. 153–57.

—— 'The Greek Fragments', in vol. 1 of *Nag Hammadi Codex II, 2–7 Together with XIII, 2*, Brit. Lib. Or.4926(1), and P.Oxy. 1, 654, 655* (ed. B. Layton; Leiden: Brill, 1989), pp. 95–128.

Baines, J., and J. Málek, *Atlas of Ancient Egypt* (Oxford: Phaidon Press, 1980).

Bartlet, V., 'The Oxyrhynchus "Sayings of Jesus"', *Contemporary Review* 87 (1905), pp. 116–25.

Bell, H. I., and T. C. Skeat, *Fragments of an Unknown Gospel and Other Early Christian Papyri* (London: Oxford University Press, 1935).

—— *The New Gospel Fragments* (London: Oxford University Press, 1935).

Berger, K., and C. Nord, *Das Neue Testament und frühchristliche Schriften* (Leipzig: Insel Verlag, 1999).

Bickell, G., 'Ein Papyrusfragment eines nichtkanonischen Evangeliums', *ZKT* 9 (1885), pp. 498–504; 10 (1886), pp. 208–09.

—— 'Das nichtkanonische Evangelienfragment', in vol. 1 of *Mittheilungen aus der Sammlung der Papyrus Erzherzog Rainer* (ed. J. Karabacek; Vienna: Verlag der k.k. Hof- und Staatsdruckerei, 1887), pp. 53–61.

—— 'Zum Evangelienfragment Raineri', in vols. 2–3 of *Mittheilungen aus der Sammlung der Papyrus Erzherzog Rainer* (ed. J. Karabacek; Vienna: Verlag der k.k. Hof- und Staatsdruckerei, 1887), pp. 41–42.

—— 'Ein letztes Wort über das Papyrusevangelium', in vol. 5 of *Mittheilungen aus der Sammlung der Papyrus Erzherzog Rainer* (ed. J. Karabacek; Vienna: Verlag der k.k. Hof- und Staatsdruckerei, 1892), pp. 78–82.

Blass, F., 'Das neue Logia-Fragment von Oxyrhynchos', *Evangelische Kirchenzeitung* (Berlin: August 8, 1897), pp. 498–500.

—— and A. Debrunner, *A Greek Grammar of the New Testament and Other Early Christian Literature* (trans. R. W. Funk; Chicago, IL: University of Chicago Press, 1961).

Bonaccorsi, G. (ed.), *Vangeli apocrifi* (Firenze: Libreria editrice fiorentina, 1948).

Bouriant, U., *Fragments du texte grec du livre d'Énoch et de quelques écrits attribués à saint Pierre* (MMAF, 9.1; Paris: Ernest Leroux, 1892).

Bovon, F., 'Fragment Oxyrhynchus 840, Fragment of a Lost Gospel, Witness of an Early Christian Controversy over Purity', *JBL* 119 (2000), pp. 705–28.

Bruston, C., 'De quelques textes difficiles de l'Évangile de Pierre', *REG* 10 (1897), pp. 58–65.

—— *Fragments d'un ancien recueil de paroles de Jésus* (Paris: Librairie Fischbacher, 1905).

Cameron, R. (ed.), *The Other Gospels: Non-Canonical Gospel Texts* (Philadelphia, PA: Westminster Press, 1982).

Cavallo, G., and H. Maehler, *Greek Bookhands of the Early Byzantine Period: A.D. 300–800* (Bulletin Supplement, 47; London: University of London Institute of Classical Studies, 1987).

Coles, R. A., '2949. Fragments of an Apocryphal Gospel(?)', in vol. 41 of *The Oxyrhynchus Papyri* (eds. G. M. Browne, R. A. Coles, J. R. Rea, J. C. Shelton and E. G. Turner; London: Egypt Exploration Society, 1972), pp. 15–16.

Comfort, P. W., and D. P. Barrett (eds.), *The Text of the Earliest New Testament Greek Manuscripts* (Wheaton, IL: Tyndale House Publishers, 2001).

Crossan, J. D., *Four Other Gospels: Shadows on the Contours of the Canon* (Sonoma, CA: Polebridge Press, 1992).

Daniels, J. B., 'The Egerton Gospel: Its Place in Early Christianity' (unpublished doctoral dissertation; Claremont Graduate School, 1990).

Danker, F. W. (ed.), *A Greek-English Lexicon of the New Testament and Other Early Christian Literature* (Chicago, IL: University of Chicago Press, 3rd edn, 2000).

Dart, J., and R. Reigert, *Unearthing the Lost Words of Jesus* (Berkeley, CA: Seastone, 1998).

Ehrman, B. D., *The New Testament and Other Early Christian Writings: A Reader* (New York: Oxford University Press, 1998).

—— *Lost Scriptures: Books That Did Not Make It into the New Testament* (New York: Oxford University Press, 2003).

Elliott, J. K., *The Apocryphal New Testament* (Oxford: Clarendon Press, 1993).

Epp, E. J., 'The Oxyrhynchus New Testament Papyri: "Not without Honor Except in Their Hometown"?', *JBL* 123 (2004), pp. 5–55.

Evelyn-White, H. G., *The Sayings of Jesus from Oxyrhynchus* (Cambridge: Cambridge University Press, 1920).

Finegan, J., *Hidden Records of the Life of Jesus* (Philadelphia, PA: Pilgrim Press, 1969).

Fitzmyer, J. A., 'The Oxyrhynchus *Logoi* of Jesus and the Coptic Gospel According to Thomas', *TS* 20 (1959), pp. 505–60.

—— *Essays on the Semitic Background of the New Testament* (London: Geoffrey Chapman, 1971).

—— *The Semitic Background of the New Testament* (Grand Rapids, MI: Eerdmans, 1997).

Gallizia, U., 'Il P. Egerton 2', *Aeg* 36 (1956), pp. 29–72, 178–234.

Gebhardt, O. von, *Das Evangelium und die Apokalypse des Petrus* (Leipzig: J. C. Hinrichs'sche Buchhandlung, 1893).

Grenfell, B. P., 'The Oldest Record of Christ's Life: The First Complete Account of the Recent Finding of the "Sayings of Our Lord"', *McClure's Magazine* (October 1897), pp. 1022–30.

Grenfell, B. P., and A. S. Hunt, *ΛΟΓΙΑ ΙΗΣΟΥ: Sayings of Our Lord from an Early Greek Papyrus* (London: Henry Frowde, 1897).

—— '1. ΛΟΓΙΑ ΙΗΣΟΥ', in vol. 1 of *The Oxyrhynchus Papyri* (London: Egypt Exploration Fund, 1898), pp. 1–3.

—— '210. Early Christian Fragment', in vol. 2 of *The Oxyrhynchus Papyri* (London: Egypt Exploration Fund, 1899), pp. 9–10.

—— *Catalogue général des antiquités égyptiennes du Musée du Caire: Nos. 10001–10869, Greek Papyri* (Oxford: Oxford University Press, 1903).

—— *New Sayings of Jesus and Fragment of a Lost Gospel from Oxyrhynchus* (London: Oxford University Press, 1904).

—— '654. New Sayings of Jesus', in vol. 4 of *The Oxyrhynchus Papyri* (London: Egypt Exploration Fund, 1904), pp. 1–22.

—— '655. Fragment of a Lost Gospel', in vol. 4 of *The Oxyrhynchus Papyri* (London: Egypt Exploration Fund, 1904), pp. 22–28.

—— *Fragment of an Uncanonical Gospel from Oxyrhynchus* (London: Oxford University Press, 1908).

—— '840. Fragment of an Uncanonical Gospel', in vol. 5 of *The Oxyrhynchus Papyri* (London: Egypt Exploration Fund, 1908), pp. 1–10.

—— '1224. Uncanonical Gospel', in vol. 10 of *The Oxyrhynchus Papyri* (London: Egypt Exploration Fund, 1914), pp. 1–10.

Gronewald, M., '255. Unbekanntes Evangelium oder Evangelienharmonie (Fragment aus dem "Evangelium Egerton")', in vol. 6 of *Kölner Papyri (P.Köln)* (eds. M. Gronewald, B. Kramer, K. Maresch, M. Parca and C. Römer; Opladen: Westdeutscher Verlag, 1987), pp. 136–45.

Guillaumont, A., 'Sémitismes dans les logia de Jésus retrouvés à Nag-Hamâdi', *JA* 246 (1958), pp. 113–23.

Harnack, A., *Bruchstücke des Evangeliums und der Apokalypse des Petrus* (Leipzig: J. C. Hinrichs'sche Buchhandlung, 1893).

Heinrici, G., 'Die neuen Herrensprüche', *TSK* 78 (1905), pp. 188–210.

Hilgenfeld, A., 'Kein unentdecktes Evangelium', *ZWT* 29 (1886), pp. 50–58.

—— 'Neue gnostische Logia Jesu', *ZWT* 47 (1904), pp. 567–73.

Hofius, O., 'Das koptische Thomasevangelium und die Oxyrhynchus-Papyri Nr. 1, 654 und 655', *EvT* 20 (1960), pp. 21–42.

Hombert, M., and B. A. van Groningen, 'Essai d'unification des méthodes employées dans les éditions de papyrus', *ChrEg* 7 (1932), pp. 285–87.

James, M. R., *The Apocryphal New Testament* (Oxford: Clarendon Press, 1924).

Jeremias, J., *Unknown Sayings of Jesus* (trans. R. H. Fuller; London: Society for Promoting Christian Knowledge, 1957).

Kasser, R., *L'Évangile selon Thomas: Présentation et commentaire théologique* (Neuchâtel: Delachaux & Niestlé, 1961).

Kloppenborg, J. S., M. W. Meyer, S. J. Patterson and M. G. Steinhauser, *Q-Thomas Reader* (Sonoma, CA: Polebridge Press, 1990).

Koester, H., 'Apocryphal and Canonical Gospels', *HTR* 73 (1980), pp. 105–30.

—— *Ancient Christian Gospels: Their History and Development* (Philadelphia, PA: Trinity Press International, 1990).

Kraft, R. A., 'Oxyrhynchus Papyrus 655 Reconsidered', *HTR* 54 (1961), pp. 253–62.

Kraus, T. J., 'P.Vindob.G 2325: Das sogenannte Fayûm-Evangelium – Neuedition und kritische Rückschlüsse', *ZAC* 5 (2001), pp. 197–212.

—— and T. Nicklas, *Das Petrusevangelium und die Petrusapokalypse: Die griechischen Fragmente mit deutscher und englischer Übersetzung* (Berlin: Walter de Gruyter, 2004).

Kruger, M. J., *Gospel of the Savior: An Analysis of P. Oxy. 840 and its Place in the Gospel Traditions of Early Christianity* (eds. S. E. Porter and W. J. Porter; Texts and Editions for New Testament Study, 1; Leiden: Brill, 2005).

Lake, K., 'The New Sayings of Jesus and the Synoptic Problem', *HibJ* 3 (1904–1905), pp. 332–41.

Lampe, G. W. H. (ed.), *A Patristic Greek Lexicon* (Oxford: Clarendon Press, 1961).

Liddell, H. G., R. Scott and H. S. Jones (eds.), *A Greek-English Lexicon* (Oxford: Clarendon Press, 9th edn, 1996).

Lietzmann, H., 'Ein apokryphes Evangelienfragment', *ZNW* 22 (1923), pp. 153–54.

Lock, W., and W. Sanday, *Two Lectures on the "Sayings of Jesus" Recently Discovered at Oxyrhynchus* (Oxford: Clarendon Press, 1897).

Lods, A., *Reproduction en héliogravure du manuscrit d'Énoch et des écrits attribués à saint Pierre* (MMAF, 9.3; Paris: Ernest Leroux, 1893).

Louw, J. P., and E. A. Nida (eds.), *Greek-English Lexicon of the New Testament Based on Semantic Domains* (2 vols.; New York: United Bible Societies, 2nd edn, 1989).

Lührmann, D., 'POx 2949: EvPt 3–5 in einer Handschrift des 2./3. Jahrhunderts', *ZNW* 72 (1981), pp. 216–26.

—— 'Die Geschichte von einer Sünderin und andere apokryphe Jesusüberlieferungen bei Didymos von Alexandrien', *NovT* 32 (1990), pp. 289–316.

—— 'POx 4009: Ein neues Fragment des Petrusevangeliums?', *NovT* 35 (1993), pp. 390–410.

—— and P. J. Parsons, '4009.Gospel of Peter?', in vol. 60 of *The Oxyrhynchus Papyri* (eds. R. A. Coles, M. W. Haslam, and P. J. Parsons; London: Egypt Exploration Society, 1994), pp. 1–5.

—— and E. Schlarb, *Fragmente apokryph gewordener Evangelien in griechischer und lateinischer Sprache* (Marburger theologische Studien, 59; Marburg: N. G. Elwert Verlag, 2000).

—— *Die apokryph gewordenen Evangelien: Studien zu neuen Texten und zu neuen Fragen* (Leiden: Brill, 2004).

MacLennan, H., *Oxyrhynchus: An Economic and Social Study* (Chicago, IL: Argonaut, Inc., Publishers, 1967).

Manchot, K., 'Die neuen Petrus-Fragmente', *Protestantische Kirchenzeitung für das evangelische Deutschland* (Berlin: February 8, 1893), pp. 126–43, 176–83, 201–13.

Marcovich, M., 'Textual Criticism on the Gospel of Thomas', *JTS* 20 (1969), pp. 53–74.

Mayeda, G., *Das Leben-Jesu-Fragment: Papyrus Egerton 2 und seine Stellung in der urchristlichen Literaturgeschichte* (Bern: Verlag Paul Haupt, 1946).

Meyer, M., *The Gospel of Thomas: The Hidden Sayings of Jesus* (San Francisco, CA: HarperSanFrancisco, 1992).

—— *The Unknown Sayings of Jesus* (San Francisco, CA: HarperSanFrancisco, 1998).

Michelsen, J. H. A., 'Nieuw-ontdekte fragmenten van evangeliën', *Teyler's theologisch tijdschrift* 3 (1905), pp. 153–64.

Miller, R. J. (ed.), *The Complete Gospels: Annotated Scholars Version* (Sonoma, CA: Polebridge Press, rev. and exp. edn, 1994).

Nations, A. L., 'A Critical Study of the Coptic Gospel According to Thomas' (unpublished doctoral dissertation; Vanderbilt University, 1960).

Oates, J. F., R. S. Bagnall, S. J. Clackson, A. A. O'Brien, J. D. Sosin, T. G. Wilfong and K. A. Worp, *Checklist of Editions of Greek, Latin, Demotic and Coptic Papyri, Ostraca and Tablets* (BASPSup, 9; Oakville, CT: American Society of Papyrologists, 5th edn, 2001).

Pesce, M. (ed.), *Le parole dimenticate di Gesù* (Milan: Fondazione Lorenzo Valla/ Arnoldo Mondadori Editore, 2004).

Porter, S. E., 'The Greek Apocryphal Gospels Papyri: The Need for a Critical Edition', in vol. 2 of *Akten des 21. Internationalen Papyrologenkongresses: Berlin, 13.-19.8.1995* (eds. B. Kramer, W. Luppe, H. Maehler and G. Poethke; Stuttgart: B. G. Teubner, 1997), pp. 795–803.

—— 'POxy II 210 as an Apocryphal Gospel and the Development of Egyptian Christianity', in vol. 2 of *Atti del XXII Congresso internazionale di papirologia: Firenze, 23–29 agosto 1998* (eds. I. Andorlini, G. Bastianini, M. Manfredi and G. Menci; Firenze: Istituto papirologico 'G. Vitelli', 2001), pp. 1095–1108.

Puech, H.-C., 'Une collection de paroles de Jésus récemment retrouvée: L'Évangile selon Thomas', *CRAIBL* (1957), pp. 146–66.

Rees, B. R., '51.Christian Fragment', in vol. 2 of *A Descriptive Catalogue of the Greek Papyri in the Collection of Wilfred Merton, F.S.A.* (eds. B. R. Rees, H. I. Bell and J. W. B. Barns; Dublin: Hodges Figgis & Co., 1959), pp. 1–4.

Roberts, C. H. (ed.), *An Unpublished Fragment of the Fourth Gospel in the John Rylands Library* (Manchester: Manchester University Press, 1935).

—— 'An Early Christian Papyrus', in *Miscellània papirològica Ramon Roca-Puig* (ed. S. Janeras; Barcelona: Fundació Salvador Vives Casajuana, 1987), pp. 293–96.

Robinson, J. A. T., and M. R. James, *The Gospel According to Peter, and the Revelation of Peter: Two Lectures on the Newly Recovered Fragments Together with the Greek Texts* (London: C. J. Clay and Sons, 1892).

Robinson, J. M. (ed.), *The Nag Hammadi Library in English* (San Francisco, CA: HarperSanFrancisco, 3rd rev. edn, 1990).

Santos Otero, A. de, *Los evangelios apócrifos: Colección de textos griegos y latinos, versión crítica, estudios introductorios, comentarios e ilustraciones* (Madrid: Biblioteca de autores cristianos, 10th edn, 1999).

Schmidt, A., 'P. Oxy. X 1224, Fragment 2 Recto, Col. I: Ein neuer Vorschlag', *ZNW* 80 (1989), pp. 276–77.

Schneemelcher, W. (ed.), *New Testament Apocrypha* (trans. R. M. Wilson; 2 vols.; Louisville, KY: Westminster/John Knox Press, rev. edn, 1991–1992).

Smyth, H. W., *Greek Grammar* (ed. G. M. Messing; Cambridge, MA.: Harvard University Press, rev. edn, 1956).

Stroker, W. D., *Extracanonical Sayings of Jesus* (Atlanta, GA: Scholars Press, 1989).

Swete, H. B., *The Apocryphal Gospel of Peter: The Greek Text of the Newly Discovered Fragment* (London: Macmillan and Co., 1892).

—— 'The New Oxyrhynchus Sayings: A Tentative Interpretation', *ExpTim* 15 (1904), pp. 488–95.

—— (ed.), *Zwei neue Evangelienfragmente* (KlT, 31; Bonn: A. Marcus und E. Weber, 1908).

Taylor, C., *The Oxyrhynchus Sayings of Jesus Found in 1903 with the Sayings Called "Logia" Found in 1897: A Lecture* (Oxford: Clarendon Press, 1905).

Turner, E. G., *The Terms Recto and Verso; The Anatomy of the Papyrus Roll* (Brussels: Fondation égyptologique Reine Élisabeth, 1978).

—— *Greek Papyri: An Introduction* (Oxford: Clarendon Press, rev. edn, 1980).

—— 'The Graeco-Roman Branch', in *Excavating in Egypt: The Egypt Exploration Society 1882–1982* (ed. T. G. H. James; Chicago, IL: University of Chicago Press, 1982), pp. 161–78.

—— *Greek Manuscripts of the Ancient World* (ed. P. J. Parsons; Bulletin Supplement, 46; London: University of London Institute of Classical Studies, 2nd edn, 1987).

Usener, H., *Religionsgeschichtliche Untersuchungen* (3 vols.; Bonn: M. Cohen & Sohn, 1889–1899).

van Groningen, B. A., 'Fragmenten van een nieuw evangelie', *Nieuwe theologische studiën* 3 (1935), pp. 210–14.

van Haelst, J., *Catalogue des papyrus littéraires juifs et chrétiens* (Paris: Publications de la Sorbonne, 1976).

van Minnen, P., 'The Greek Apocalypse of Peter', in *The Apocalypse of Peter* (eds. J. N. Bremmer and I. Czachesz; Studies on Early Christian Apocrypha, 7; Leuven: Peeters, 2003).

Vielhauer, P., *Geschichte der urchristlichen Literatur: Einleitung in das Neue Testament, die Apokryphen und die Apostolischen Väter* (Berlin: Walter de Gruyter, 1975).

Wessely, C., *Les plus anciens monuments du christianisme écrits sur papyrus* (PO, 4.2; Paris: Firmin-Didot, 1906).

West, M. L., *Textual Criticism and Editorial Technique Applicable to Greek and Latin Texts* (Stuttgart: B. G. Teubner, 1973).

Zahn, T., 'Neue Funde aus der alten Kirche', *NKZ* 16 (1905), pp. 94–101, 165–78.

INDEXES

THE GOSPEL OF THOMAS

Oxyrhynchus Papyri 654, 1, 655 (P.Oxy. 654, 1, 655)

Note: 1(2) means 'saying 1, line 2'

ἀδελφός 26(4)
ἄθεος 30(3)*
αἰσχύνω 37(23)
ἀκέραιος 39(21)*
ἀκούω 33(20)
ἄκρον 32(16)
ἀλήθεια 6(38)*
ἄν 1(3)*, 2(6)*, 3(16)*, 36(13)
ἀνάθεμα 7(42)ᵃᵖ
ἀναπαύω 2(8)*
ἄνθρωπος 4(22)*, 7(41)*, 7(41)*, 7(42)*, 28(19)
ἀπό 5(29), 36(1)*, 36(2)
ἀποκαλύπτω 5(29)*
ἀποκνέω 4(22)
ἀποκρύπτω 6(39)*
ἀπόκρυφος Pro(1)*
αὐξάνω 36(9)ᵃᵖ
αὐτός 4(24)*, 6(32), 6(32)*, 28(14), 28(17), 28(21)*, 30(5)*, 31(11)*, 31(14), 36(15)*, 37(17), 37(18), 39(16)*
ἀφίημι 39(18)*

β′ 30(3)ᵃᵖ
βασιλεία 3(11), 3(15)*, 27(7)
βασιλεύω 2(8), 2(8)*
βλέπω 28(21)*
βρῶμα 6(35)*

γ′ 30(3)ᵃᵖ
γάρ 5(29)*, 6(39)*

γεύομαι 1(5)
γῆ 3(13)
γίνομαι 5(30)*, 39(20)*
γινώσκω 3(17), 3(18), 3(20), 5(27)*, 31(14)
γνῶσις 39(15)*
γραμματεύς 39(13)*
γράφω Pro(2)*

δέ 3(12)*, 3(19)*, 39(20)
δεκτός 31(10)
διαβλέπω 26(1)
δίδωμι 36(15)*
διψάω 28(16)
δύναμαι 32(19)
δύο 30(3)ᵃᵖ

ἐάν 3(9)*, 3(12)*, 27(5), 27(8), 30(2)
ἑαυτοῦ 3(16)*, 3(18), 3(20)
ἐγείρω 5(31)*, 77(6)*
ἐγώ 28(18), 30(5), 77(7), 77(8), 37(19)
εἰ 3(19)*
εἶδον 3(18)ᵃᵖ
εἰμί 3(13)*, 3(16)*, 3(19), 3(20)*, 3(21), 4(25), 5(27)*, 5(29)*, 6(39)*, 6(40)*, 7(40), 7(41)*, 24(1)*, 24(5)*, 28(20), 30(2), 30(3)*, 30(4), 30(5), 77(9), 31(10), 36(8)*, 37(20)
εἶπον 1(3), 3(10)*, 3(12)*
εἰς 4(26)*, 31(13), 33(21)*
εἷς 4(26)*, 30(4)*, 33(21)*
εἰσέρχομαι 39(17)*, 39(18)*, 39(19)*
ἐκβάλλω 26(2)

ἐκδύω 37(22)
ἐκεῖ 77(7), 77(9)
ἐκτός 3(16)*
ἐλεημοσύνη 6(34)*
ἕλκω 3(10)
ἔμπροσθεν 5(27)*
ἐμφανής 37(19)
ἐν 3(11), 3(20), 26(3), 28(12), 28(13),
  28(17), 31(11)
ἐνδέω 36(12)ᵃᵖ
ἔνδυμα 36(11)*, 36(16)
ἐνδύω 36(6)*, 36(12)*
ἐνοικέω 29(0)*
ἐντός 3(16)
ἐξετάζω 6(32)*
ἐπερωτάω 4(23)
ἐπί 28(18), 32(16), 36(14)
ἑπτά 4(23)*
ἑρμηνεία 1(3)*
ἐσθίω 7(40)*, 7(42)*, 36(4)*
ἑσπέρα 36(2)*
ἔσχατος 4(25)*, 4(26)
εὑρίσκω 1(4)*, 2(7), 2(7), 3(17)*, 27(7),
  28(14), 28(16), 77(7)
ἔχω 36(11)*
ἕως 2(6)*, 36(1)*, 36(3)*

ζάω Pro(2), 3(19)*, 4(24)*
ζητέω 2(6)*, 2(6)*
ζωή 4(24)*

ἡλικία 36(14)
ἡμέρα 4(22)*, 4(23)*

θάλασσα 3(14)*
θαμβέω 2(7)*, 2(7)*
θάνατος 1(4)*
θάπτω 5(31)
θεός 27(8)
θεραπεία 31(13)

ἰατρός 31(12)
ἰδού 3(10)*
ἵστημι 28(11)*
ἰχθύς 3(14)

καλύπτω 5(28)*
καρδία 28(20)

κάρφος 26(2)
καταντάω 4(26)*
κλείς 39(14)*
κόσμος 24(3)*, 27(6), 28(12)
κρείσσων 36(7)*
κρίνον 36(8)*
κρυπτός 5(30)
κρύπτω 32(19)*, 39(15)*

λαλέω Pro(1)*
λαμβάνω 39(14)*
λέγω 2(5)*, 3(9), 4(21)*, 5(27), 6(33)*,
  6(36), 27(4), 28(11), 30(2)*, 30(5)*,
  31(9), 32(15), 33(20), 36(0)*, 37(17),
  37(21), 38(2)*, 39(12)*
λέων 7(40)*, 7(41)*, 7(42)*
λίθος 77(6)
λόγος Pro(1), 1(4)

μαθητής 6(32)*, 37(18)
μακάριος 7(40)*
μεθύω 28(15)
μεριμνάω 36(0)*
μέσος 28(12)
μετά 30(5)
μή 1(5), 2(6), 3(19)*, 6(36)*, 6(37),
  27(5), 27(6), 27(8), 36(0)*, 37(23)
μηδείς 36(10)*
μήτε 36(2)*, 36(3), 36(5)*
μισέω 6(37)*
μόνος 30(4)

νήθω 36(10)*
νηστεύω 6(33)*, 27(5)

ξαίνω 36(9)*
ξύλον 77(8)

οἶδα 3(18)*
οἰκοδομέω 32(15)
ὅπου 30(2)*, 30(4)*
ὁράω 27(10), 28(13), 37(21)
ὅρος 32(17)*
ὅς Pro(1)*, 5(30), 5(31), 6(39)*, 7(40)*,
  7(42)*, 33(20)*
ὅστις 1(3)*, 3(16)*, 6(36)*, 36(9)*
ὅταν 2(7), 37(22)
ὅτε 3(17)*

ὅτι 3(12)*, 3(18)*, 4(25), 28(20)
οὐ 1(5), 4(22), 5(29)*, 5(30), 5(31)*,
    6(39)*, 27(6), 27(10), 28(21)*, 31(9),
    36(9)*
οὐαί 7(42)*
οὐδέ 31(12), 36(10)*
οὐδείς 6(38)*, 28(16)
οὐρανός 3(11)*, 3(12)*
οὔτε 32(18), 32(19), 39(16)*, 39(17)*
οὗτος Pro(1), 1(4)*, 3(17), 29(1)*
ὀφθαλμός 26(3)
ὄφις 39(21)*
ὀψέ 36(1)*
ὄψις 5(28)

παιδίον 4(23)*
παλαιός 4(22)*
παρατηρέω 6(35)*
πᾶς 28(14)
πατήρ 3(15)*, 3(19), 27(11)
πατρίς 31(11)
παύω 2(6)
περί 4(24), 6(35)*
περιστερά 39(22)*
πετεινόν 3(12)
πίπτω 32(18)*
πλήρης 4(22)ᵃᵖ
ποιέω 6(34)*, 6(37)*, 31(12)
πόλις 32(15)
πολύς 4(25), 36(7)*
πονέω 28(17)
πότε 37(19), 37(20)
προσεύχομαι 6(33)*
προστίθημι 36(13)*
προφήτης 31(10)
πρωῒ 36(1), 36(3)*
πρῶτος 4(25)*, 4(26)

πτωχεία 3(20)*, 3(21)*, 29(1)
πῶς 6(33), 6(33)*, 6(34)

σαββατίζω 27(9)
σάββατον 27(9)
σάρξ 28(13)
στηρίζω 32(17)
στολή 36(5)*
σύ 3(10), 3(10)*, 3(11)*, 3(15), 3(16),
    3(17)*, 3(19), 3(21), 5(28), 5(29),
    5(29)*, 26(4), 33(21), 36(4)*, 36(6)*,
    36(13), 36(15), 36(16), 36(16), 37(21),
    39(19)*
σχίζω 77(8)

τίς 6(35), 36(4), 36(6)*, 36(12)*, 36(13)
τοῖος Pro(1)ᵃᵖ
τόπος 4(24)
τότε 26(1)
τρεῖς 30(3)*
τροφή 36(4)*
τυφλός 28(20)

υἱός 3(18)*, 28(19)
ὑπό 3(13)
ὑψηλός 32(17)

φανερός 5(30)*, 6(39)*
φθάνω 3(11)*
φρόνιμος 39(20)*
φωτεινός 24(2)*

ψεύδομαι 6(36)*
ψυχή 28(18)

ὡς 39(21)*, 39(22)*
ὠτίον 33(21)*

Proper names

Θωμᾶς Pro(3)

Ἰησοῦς Pro(2), 2(5)*, 3(9)*, 4(21)*,
    5(27), 6(36), 27(5), 28(11), 30(2)*,

    31(9), 32(15), 33(20), 36(0)*, 38(2)*,
    39(12)*
Ἰούδας Pro(2)*

Φαρισαῖος 39(12)*

THE GOSPEL OF PETER

Oxyrhynchus Papyrus 4009 (P.Oxy. 4009)

ἀκέραιος (→).5*
ἀνά (→).8*
ἀπό (→).16*
ἀποκρίνομαι (→).11*
ἀποκτείνω (→).16*, (→).18*
ἀρνίον (→).8*, (→).13*
αὐτός (→).9*, (→).13*, (↓).10
ἀφίημι (↓).13*

γίνομαι (→).5*

δέ (→).5*, (→).11*
διό (→).14*
δύναμαι (→).14*, (→).19*

ἐάν (→).9
ἐγώ (→).11, (→).15*
εἰμί (→).7
εἶπον (→).9*
ἔχω (→).20*

θερισμός (→).4

κύριος (↓).13

λέγω (→).11, (→).15*

λύκος (→).8*, (→).12*

μέσος (→).8*
μετά (→).17*
μή (→).15*
μηδείς (→).19*
μηκέτι (→).18*

ὅτι (↓).8
οὐδέ (↓).4*
οὐδείς (→).13*
οὐκέτι (→).13*
οὖν (→).9
ὄφις (→).7*

περιστερά (→).5*
ποιέω (→).14*, (→).18*
πρός (→).9*

σπαράσσω (→).10*, (→).12*
σύ (→).15*, (→).17*

φοβέω (→).15*
φρόνιμος (→).6*

ὡς (→).5, (→).7*, (→).7*

The Akhmim Fragment (P.Cair. 10759)

ἀγαθός 6.23
ἀγανακτέω 4.14
ἀγαπάω 12.50

ἀγωνιάω 5.15, 11.45
ἀδελφός 2.5, 14.60
ἀδικέω 4.13

ἄζυμος 2.5, 14.58
αἷμα 11.46
αἰτέω 2.3, 2.4, 2.5
ἀκάνθινος 3.8
ἀκολουθέω 10.39
ἀκούω 8.28, 10.41, 10.42
ἀληθῶς 11.45
ἀλλήλων 8.28, 11.43
ἄλλος 3.9
ἁμάρτημα 5.17
ἁμαρτία 7.25, 11.48
ἀμφότεροι 9.37
ἄν 12.52, 12.54
ἀνά 4.10, 9.35
ἀναβοάω 5.19
ἀναλαμβάνω 5.19
ἀναπαύω 5.18ᵃᵖ
ἀνήρ 9.36, 10.39
ἄνθρωπος 4.13, 11.44
ἀνίστημι 1.1*, 8.30, 13.56, 13.56
ἀνοίγω 9.36, 9.37, 11.44, 13.55
ἀπαλλάσσω 14.59
ἅπας 8.28
ἀπέρχομαι 11.43, 13.55, 13.56,
    13.56, 14.60
ἀπό 6.21, 9.34, 9.37, 10.39,
    10.42
ἀποθνήσκω 4.14, 12.50
ἀποκρίνομαι 11.46
ἀποκυλίω 12.53
ἀποσπάω 6.21
ἀποστέλλω 13.56
ἄρχω 7.25
αὐτός 1.1, 1.2, 1.2, 2.3, 2.4, 2.5, 2.5,
    2.5, 2.5, 3.6, 3.6, 3.7, 3.7, 3.8, 3.9, 3.9,
    3.9, 3.9, 4.10, 4.10, 4.12, 4.12, 4.13,
    4.14, 5.15, 5.16, 5.16, 5.17, 5.20, 6.21,
    6.23, 6.23, 7.26, 8.28, 8.29, 8.30, 8.30,
    8.30, 8.31, 8.31, 10.38, 10.39, 10.39,
    10.40, 11.44, 11.47, 12.50, 12.52,
    12.52, 12.53, 12.54, 13.55, 14.58,
    14.59
ἀφίημι 11.45

βάλλω 4.12, 9.37, 12.54
βασανίζω 4.14
βασιλεύς 1.2, 3.7, 4.11
βούλομαι 1.1*

γάρ 2.5, 5.15*, 7.26, 10.38, 11.48, 12.54,
    13.56
γῆ 6.21, 6.21
γίνομαι 4.13, 6.21, 8.28, 9.35
γινώσκω 7.25
γογγύζω 8.28
γραμματεύς 8.28, 8.31
γράφω 2.5, 5.15
γυνή 12.50, 13.57

δέ 1.1, 2.3, 3.6, 4.10, 4.13, 4.13, 5.15,
    5.18, 6.23, 6.24, 7.26, 7.27, 8.28,
    8.31, 9.34, 9.35, 9.37, 10.40, 11.46,
    12.50, 12.53, 13.56, 14.58, 14.59,
    14.60
δέομαι 8.29, 11.47
διά 4.13, 12.50, 14.59
διαμερίζω 4.12
διανοέομαι 11.44
διάνοια 7.26
διαρρήγνυμι 5.20
δίδωμι 6.23
δίκαιος 8.28
δικαίως 3.7
δοκέω 11.46
δύναμαι 12.52, 12.54
δύναμις 5.19, 5.19
δύνω 2.5, 5.15, 5.15
δύο 4.10, 5.20, 9.35, 9.35, 9.36, 10.39,
    10.40
δώδεκα 14.59

ἑαυτοῦ 7.25, 9.37, 12.51
ἐγγίζω 7.25, 9.36
ἐγώ 2.5, 4.13, 5.19, 5.19, 7.25, 7.26,
    7.26, 8.30, 8.30, 11.46, 11.48, 12.53,
    12.54, 12.54, 14.59, 14.60, 14.60,
    14.60, 14.60
εἰ 2.5, 8.28, 12.52, 12.54, 13.56
εἶδον 8.28, 9.34, 9.36, 10.38, 10.39,
    11.45, 11.45, 11.47, 12.52, 12.54,
    13.56
εἰμί 4.11, 5.15, 5.18, 6.23, 8.28, 8.32,
    11.45, 12.51, 12.54, 13.56, 14.58, 14.60
εἶπον 1.2, 5.16, 5.19, 11.47, 11.49
εἰς 5.20, 6.24, 11.44, 11.48, 12.54,
    12.54, 14.58, 14.59, 14.60
εἷς 2.5, 4.13, 10.39

κύριος 1.2, 2.3, 2.3, 3.6, 3.8, 4.10, 5.19,
   6.21, 6.24, 12.50, 12.50, 14.59, 14.60

λαμβάνω 3.6, 6.24, 12.51, 14.60
λαμπρός 13.55
λάμπω 6.22
λαός 2.5, 8.28, 8.30, 11.48
λαχμός 4.12
λέγω 3.6, 3.7, 3.9, 4.13, 5.19, 7.25, 8.28,
   8.29, 10.41, 11.45, 12.52
λιθάζω 11.48
λίθος 8.32, 9.37, 12.53, 12.54
λίνον 14.60
λούω 6.24
λυπέω 7.26, 14.59, 14.59
λύχνος 5.18

μαθητής 8.30, 14.59
μαθήτρια 12.50
μαστίζω 3.9
μεγάλως 11.45
μέγας 6.21, 8.28, 8.32, 9.35, 11.48,
   12.54
μέλλω 2.3
μέν 10.40
μέρος 9.37
μεσημβρία 5.15
μέσος 4.10, 13.55
μετά 5.16, 5.18, 7.26, 8.31, 8.32,
   12.51
μέχρι 10.40
μή 1.1*, 2.5, 2.5, 4.14, 5.15, 11.48,
   12.52, 12.52, 12.54, 12.54, 13.56,
   13.56
μηδείς 4.10, 11.47, 11.49
μήποτε 5.15, 8.30
μνῆμα 8.30, 8.31, 8.32, 11.44, 12.50,
   12.52
μνημεῖον 9.34, 12.51, 12.53
μνημοσύνη 12.54

ναί 10.42
ναός 5.20, 7.26
νεανίσκος 9.37, 13.55
νεκρός 8.30
νηστεύω 7.27
νίπτω 1.1, 1.1
νομίζω 5.18

νόμος 2.5
νῦν 12.52
νύξ 5.18, 7.27, 9.35, 11.45
νύσσω 3.9

ὅθεν 13.56
οἶδα 2.3
οἶκος 12.54, 14.58, 14.59
οἷος 7.25
ὁμοῦ 8.32
ὀνειδίζω 4.13
ὄξος 5.16
ὅπου 12.51
ὅπως 4.14
ὁράω 10.39, 13.55
ὀργή 12.50
ὀρθόω 4.11
ὄρθρος 12.50
ὅς 4.13, 9.35, 10.39, 11.45, 11.47, 12.50,
   12.52, 12.54, 14.60
ὅσος 1.2, 6.23
ὅσπερ 11.45
ὅστις 13.55
ὅτε 4.11
ὅτι 1.2, 2.3, 4.11, 5.18, 8.28, 8.28, 8.28,
   8.30, 10.42, 13.56
οὐ 12.50, 13.56
οὐαί 7.25
οὐδέ 1.1, 1.1
οὐδείς 1.1
οὖν 10.38, 11.43, 11.49
οὐρανός 9.35, 9.36*, 10.40, 10.40,
   10.41, 11.44
οὗτος 3.9, 4.11, 4.13, 7.27, 8.28, 11.43,
   11.45, 11.46, 12.52
οὕτω 4.13
ὀφείλω 12.53
ὀφλισκάνω 11.48
ὄχλος 9.34
ὄψις 3.9

πάλιν 10.39, 11.44
παρά 9.37
παραδίδωμι 2.5, 8.30, 8.31
παρακαθίζω 12.53
παρακαλέω 11.47
παρακύπτω 13.55, 13.56
παραλαμβάνω 1.2*

φοβέω 8.29, 12.50, 12.52, 12.54, 13.57
φόβος 6.21
φονεύω 2.5, 5.15
φρουρά 9.35
φυλάσσω 8.30, 8.31, 8.33, 9.35, 10.38, 11.45
φωνή 9.35, 10.41

χαίρω 6.23

χείρ 1.1, 6.21, 11.48
χειραγωγέω 10.40
χολή 5.16
χωρέω 10.40

ὠθέω 3.6
ὥρα 5.20, 6.22
ὡραῖος 13.55
ὡς 4.10, 7.26, 7.26

Proper names

Ἀλφαῖος 14.60
Ἀνδρέας 14.60

Ἡρῴδης 1.1, 1.2, 2.4, 2.5

Ἰερουσαλήμ 5.20, 7.25, 9.34
Ἰουδαῖος 1.1, 5.15, 6.23, 7.25, 11.48, 12.50, 12.52
Ἰσραήλ 3.7, 4.11
Ἰωσήφ 2.3, 6.23, 6.24

Λευείς 14.60

Μαγδαληνή 12.50
Μαριάμ 12.50

Πειλᾶτος 1.1, 2.3, 2.3, 2.4, 2.5, 8.29, 8.31, 11.43, 11.45, 11.46, 11.49

Πέτρος 14.60
Πετρώνιος 8.31

Σίμων 14.60

Φαρισαῖος 8.28

Oxyrhynchus Papyrus 2949 (*P.Oxy. 2949*)

ἀδελφός 2.2*
αἰτέω 1.7*, 1.9*, 1.11*, 2.3*
ἀποδίδωμι 1.10*
αὐτός 1.9*, 1.12, 2.3*, 2.4*

δέ 1.4*

ἐγώ 2.2*, 2.3*
εἰ 2.2*
εἶπον 1.10*
εἰς 1.8
ἐκεῖ 1.4*
ἔρχομαι 1.7*

θάπτω 2.3*

ἵστημι 1.4*

κελεύω 1.6
κύριος 1.5*, 1.8*

μή 2.2*

οἶδα 1.6*
ὅτι 1.6, 1.13

πέμπω 1.9*
πρός 1.7, 1.9*

σταυρόω 1.6*
σῶμα 1.8, 1.10*

ταφή 1.8
τὶς 2.3

φίλος 1.5

Indexes

Proper names

Ἡρῴδης 1.9*

Ἰωσήφ 1.5*

Πειλᾶτος 1.5*, 1.7*, 1.8*, 2.2*

EGERTON PAPYRUS 2: THE UNKNOWN GOSPEL

Egerton Papyrus 2 (P.Egerton 2) with Cologne Papyrus 255 (P.Köln. 255)

στόμα 2(→).10*
στρέφω 1(↓).6*
σύ 1(↓).8, 1(↓).12*, 1(↓).13, 1(↓).14*,
  1(↓).16, 1(↓).19*, 1(↓).23*, 1(→).15*,
  2(→).11*, 2(→).12*
συνεσθίω 1(→).13*
συνοδεύω 1(→).12*

τιμάω 2(→).14*
τίς 2(→).10
τόπος 2(↓).1*
τότε 2(↓).11

ὕδωρ 2(↓).12*
ὑπέρ 2(→).5
ὑπό 1(↓).19
ὑποτάσσω 2(↓).2*

φημί 1(→).16*

χεῖλος 2(→).14*, 2(↓).7
χείρ 1(→).4*, 1(→).9*, 2(↓).8*

ὥρα 1(→).8
ὡς 1(→).22*, 2(↓).5*

Proper names

Ἠσαΐας 2(→).12*

Ἰησοῦς 1(↓).17*, 1(→).12, 1(→).19,
  2(→).3, 2(→).8, 2(↓).6

Ἰορδάνης 2(↓).7*

Μωϋσῆς 1(↓).13, 1(↓).15, 1(↓).21*,
  1(→).22*

OTHER UNIDENTIFIED GOSPEL FRAGMENTS

The Faiyum Fragment (P. Vindob. G 2325)

ἀλεκτρυών 6
ἀπαρνέομαι 7*
ἅπας 1*
αὐτός 6ᵃᵖ

γράφω 3

δέ 1*
διασκορπίζω 4*
δίς 6

ἐγώ 5*, 7*
εἰ 5
εἶπον 1*, 4*
ἐν 1*, 2*
ἐξάγω 1*

ἤ 6ᵃᵖ

κατά 3*
κοκκύζω 6*
κύριος 6ᵃᵖ

λέγω 6*

νύξ 2

ὅτι 1*
οὐ 5*
οὗτος 2*

πᾶς 5
πατάσσω 3
ποιμήν 3*
πρίν 6*
πρόβατον 4*

σκανδαλίζω 2*

τρίς 7*

φημί 6ᵃᵖ

ὡς 1

Proper names

Ἰησοῦς 6*

Πέτρος 5

Merton Papyrus 51 (P. Mert. 51)

ἀγαθός (↓).3*
ἀθετέω (→).6*, (→).7*
ἀκούω (→).2*

ἁμαρτία (→).3
ἀπόλλυμι (↓).5*
ἀποστέλλω (↓).3*

αὐτός (→).8*

βαπτίζω (→).4
βουλή (→).5*

δέ (→).4*
δένδρον (↓).2*
δικαιόω (→).2*

ἑαυτοῦ (→).3
ἐκ (↓).2, (↓).3*

θεός (→).2, (→).5, (→).6*
θησαυρός (↓).4

καρδία (↓).4*

λαός (→).1*

μετά (→).8*

ὁμολογέω (→).3*
ὅτε (↓).3
οὐ (→).4*, (↓).7

πᾶς (→).1*
ποιέω (↓).7*
πονηρός (↓).1*, (↓).2*
προφέρω (↓).1*, (↓).1*

τελώνης (→).1*

ὡς (↓).2

Proper names

Φαρισαῖος (→).4*

Oxyrhynchus Papyrus 210 (P.Oxy. 210)

ἀγαθός 1(↓).4*, 1(↓).7*, 1(↓).10*,
  1(↓).14*, 1(↓).15*, 1(↓).16, 1(↓).17*
ἄγγελος 1(→).5, 1(→).6*
ἀλλά 1(↓).12
ἄνθρωπος 1(↓).28*

δέ 1(→).4*
δένδρον 1(↓).16*
δύναμαι 1(→).3*

ἐγώ 1(→).7*, 1(↓).17*

εἰκών 1(↓).18, 1(↓).20
εἰμί 1(↓).17, 1(↓).18, 1(↓).22
ἐν 1(↓).19
ἐρῶ 1(↓).13
ἔτι 1(→).10

θεός 1(↓).12, 1(↓).14*, 1(↓).19, 1(↓).21,
  1(↓).21

καρπός 1(↓).16*

λέγω 1(↓).5

μορφή 1(↓).19

ὁρατός 1(↓).23
ὅς 1(↓).19*
ὅτι 1(↓).25
οὐ 1(→).3
οὗτος 1(→).9

πατήρ 1(↓).6
περί 1(→).6*

τάσσω 1(→).5*

ὑπό 1(↓).17
ὑπομένω 1(→).4*

φέρω 1(↓).11*, 1(↓).14*, 1(↓).15*

ὡς 1(↓).20

Proper names

Ἰησοῦς 1(↓).13*

Oxyrhynchus Papyrus 1224 (P.Oxy. 1224)

ἀγανακτέω 175.3*
ἀκούω 175.5*
ἀλλά 173.4
ἁμαρτωλός 175.3*
ἀμήν 139.2
ἀνά 175.4
ἀντίδικος 176.6*
ἀπεῖπον 174.2*
ἀποκρίνομαι 174.1*
αὔριον 176.4
αὐτός 175.2*

βαρέω 173.1

γάρ 173.3*, 176.2
γίνομαι 176.5*
γραμματεύς 175.1

δέ 175.1, 175.5*
διδάσκω 174.3*
διδαχή 174.3*

ἐγώ 173.1
εἰμί 176.2, 176.3
εἶπον 175.5*
ἐν 139.1, 173.2*, 176.5
ἐχθρός 176.2*
ἔχω 175.6*

θεάομαι 175.2*

ἰατρός 175.6*
ἱερεύς 175.2

καινός 174.3*, 174.4
κατά 176.3*
κεῖμαι 175.4*

λέγω 139.3*

μακράν 176.4
μέσος 175.4*
μή 174.1, 176.2

ὅραμα 173.2*
ὅτι 175.3*
οὐ 173.3, 175.5*

πᾶς 139.1
ποῖος 174.2*
προσεύχομαι 176.1*

σύ 139.2*, 140.1, 174.2, 176.2, 176.3*,
   176.3
σύν 175.3*

ὑγιαίνω 175.6*
ὑπέρ 176.1, 176.3

φημί 174.3*

χρεία 175.5*

Proper names

Ἰησοῦς 173.2, 175.5

Φαρισαῖος 175.1*

Oxyrhynchus Parchment 840 (P.Oxy. 840)

ἅγιος 14, 21, 29
ἁγνευτήριον 8*, 13

ἀλλά 2, 5*, 16, 45*
ἀλλάσσω 19*

ἄλλος 18*
ἀνέρχομαι 27*
ἄνθρωπος 5, 39
ἀπό 44*
ἀποκρίνομαι 22*, 30*
ἀπολαμβάνω 4*
ἀρχιερεύς 10
αὐλητρίς 36
αὐτός 3, 7, 8, 11, 22*, 24, 30

βάλλω 33*
βαπτίζω 15*, 42*
βάπτω 43*
βάσανος 7

γάρ 3, 25

δέ 39, 41
δέρμα 35
διά 25, 26

ἐγώ 41, 42*
εἰ 18*
εἶδον 13
εἰμί 17*, 23
εἶπον 11*, 31
εἰς 8
εἰσάγω 8
ἐκεῖνος 24, 39*
ἐκτός 35
ἐν 4, 9, 23, 25, 33, 43
ἔνδοθεν 39
ἔνδυμα 19*, 27
ἐνδύω 27
ἐνταῦθα 23
ἐπιθυμία 38*
ἐπιτρέπω 12
ἔρχομαι 28, 44
ἕτερος 25, 26
εὐθέως 21ᵃᵖ
εὐθύς 21ᵃᵖ

ζῷον 4ᵃᵖ
ζωός 4

ἡμέρα 34

ἱερόν 9, 17, 23

ἵστημι 21*

καθαρεύω 23, 24
καθαρός 18, 28
κακία 41*
κακοῦργος 5
καλλωπίζω 38*
κατέρχομαι 26
κλῖμαξ 26
κόλασις 6
κύων 33

λέγω 24, 42
λευκός 27
λίμνη 25
λούω 14*, 19, 24*, 32, 37

μαθητής 15, 22*, 42*
μή 2, 18*, 31, 42
μήν 15
μήτε 14, 14*
μολύνω 16*
μόνος 4
μυρίζω 36*

νίπτω 34*
νύξ 34

ὅμοιος 3
ὄνομα 11
ὁράω 20*, 31*
ὅς 18, 33, 42
ὅσπερ 35
οὐ 3
οὐαί 31, 45*
οὐδέ 20
οὐδείς 18
οὖν 23*
οὗτος 13, 13*, 17, 20*, 29, 32

παραλαμβάνω 7
πᾶς 1*, 41*
πάσχω 3
πατέω 12*, 17, 20
περιπατέω 9
πληρόω 40*
πολύς 6*
πόρνη 36

πούς 15*
προαδικέω 1*
πρός 30, 38
προσβλέπω 29
προσέρχομαι 9*
προσέχω 2
πρότερος 1
πώς 2

σκεῦος 14, 21*, 30
σκορπίος 40
σμήχω 35, 37
σοφίζω 1*
σύ 3, 12, 15, 23*, 32
σύν 22*

συντυγχάνω 11
σωτήρ 12, 21*, 30

τίς 12
τὶς 10
τολμάω 20*
τόπος 17*
τότε 28
τυφλός 31

ὕδωρ 33*, 43
ὑπομένω 6

χέω 32
χοῖρος 33

Proper names

Δαυίδ 25   Φαρισαῖος 10

Berlin Papyrus 11710 (P.Berol. 11710)

αἴρω 15
ἁμαρτία 16
ἀμνός 14
ἀποκρίνομαι 4*, 9, 18
αὐτός 4*, 10, 19

εἰμί 3, 13
εἶπον 2, 6, 12, 21
ἐν 8

ἥλιος 9

θεός 4, 15

κόσμος 17
κύριος 3, 13

πορεύω 8

ῥαββίς 2, 5, 12 , 19

σύ 3, 13

υἱός 3

Proper names

Ἰησοῦς 22
Ναθαναήλ 6, 10

Χριστός 22

Coptic words

ⲚⲞⲨⲦⲈ 22

INDEX OF REFERENCES

INDEX OF AUTHORS

PLATES

1. *P.Oxy. 654(↓).* By permission of the British Library, Papyrus 1531 (70 per cent of actual size).

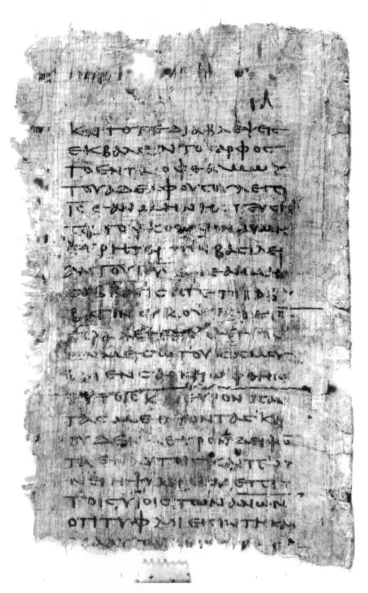

2. *P.Oxy. 1(↓)*. The Bodleian Library, University of Oxford, MS. Gr. th. e. 7(P).

3. *P.Oxy. 1(→)*. The Bodleian Library, University of Oxford, MS. Gr. th. e. 7(P).

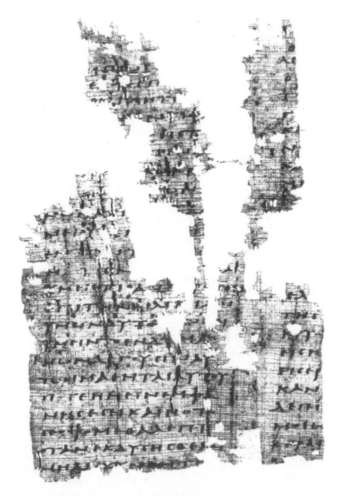

4. *P.Oxy. 655, fragments a–c.* By permission of the Houghton Library, Harvard University, SM 4367 (a–c).

5. *P.Oxy. 655, fragments d & e.* By permission of the Houghton Library, Harvard University, SM 4367 (d–e).

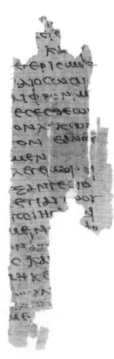

6. *P.Oxy. 4009(→)*. Courtesy of the Egypt Exploration Society.

7. *P.Oxy. 4009(↓).* Courtesy of the Egypt Exploration Society.

8. *P.Cair. 10759, page 2.* Digital image: Centre for the Study of Ancient Documents, University of Oxford from original photograph by A. Bülow-Jacobsen (AIP archive).

9. *P. Cair. 10759, page 3.* Digital image: Centre for the Study of Ancient Documents, University of Oxford from original photograph by A. Bülow-Jacobsen (AIP archive).

10. *P.Cair. 10759, page 4.* Digital image: Centre for the Study of Ancient Documents, University of Oxford from original photograph by A. Bülow-Jacobsen (AIP archive).

11. *P.Cair. 10759, page 5.* Digital image: Centre for the Study of Ancient Documents, University of Oxford from original photograph by A. Bülow-Jacobsen (AIP archive).

12. *P.Cair. 10759, page 6.* Digital image: Centre for the Study of Ancient Documents, University of Oxford from original photograph by A. Bülow-Jacobsen (AIP archive).

13. *P.Cair. 10759, page 7.* Digital image: Centre for the Study of Ancient Documents, University of Oxford from original photograph by A. Bülow-Jacobsen (AIP archive).

14. *P. Cair. 10759, page 8.* Digital image: Centre for the Study of Ancient Documents, University of Oxford from original photograph by A. Bülow-Jacobsen (AIP archive).

15. *P.Cair. 10759, page 9.* Digital image: Centre for the Study of Ancient Documents, University of Oxford from original photograph by A. Bülow-Jacobsen (AIP archive).

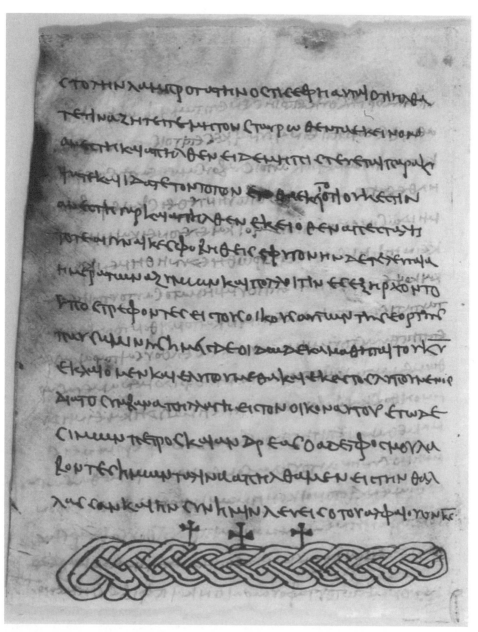

16. *P.Cair. 10759, page 10.* Digital image: Centre for the Study of Ancient Documents, University of Oxford from original photograph by A. Bülow-Jacobsen (AIP archive).

17. *P.Oxy. 2949, fragments 1 & 2*. Courtesy of the Egypt Exploration Society.

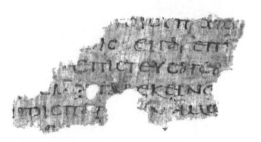

18. *P.Egerton 2, fragment 1(↓)*. By permission of the British Library, Egerton Papyrus 2.
   P.Köln 255(↓). Institut für Altertumskunde, University of Cologne, Inv. Nr. 608.

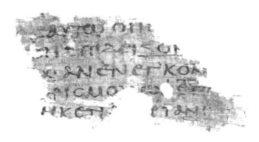

19. *P.Egerton 2, fragment 1* (→). By permission of the British Library, Egerton Papyrus 2.
   P.Köln 255(→). Institut für Altertumskunde, University of Cologne, Inv. Nr. 608.

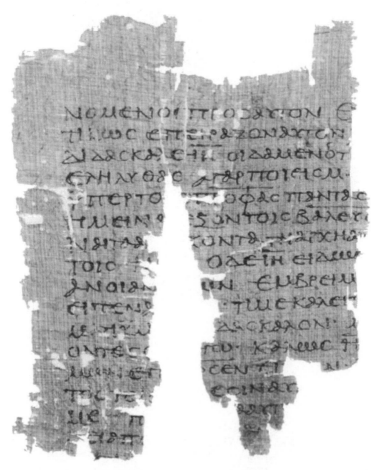

20. *P.Egerton 2, fragment 2(→)*. By permission of the British Library, Egerton Papyrus 2.

21. *P.Egerton 2, fragment 2(↓)*. By permission of the British Library, Egerton Papyrus 2.

22. *P.Egerton 2, fragment 3(↓)*. By permission of the British Library, Egerton Papyrus 2.

23. *P. Egerton 2, fragment 3(→)*. By permission of the British Library, Egerton
Papyrus 2.

24. *P.Oxy. 210, fragment 1(→)*. By permission of the Syndics of Cambridge University Library, Add. Ms. 4048.

25. *P.Oxy. 210, fragment 1(↓)*. By permission of the Syndics of Cambridge University Library, Add. Ms. 4048.

26. *P.Oxy. 1224, fragments 1(↓) & 2(→).* The Bodleian Library, University of Oxford, MS. Gr. th. e. 8(P) (cropped image).

27. *P.Oxy. 840, back.* The Bodleian Library, University of Oxford, MS. Gr. th. g. 11.

28. *P.Berol. 11710, fragment a(↓)*. Staatliche Museen zu Berlin Preußischer Kulturbesitz, Papyrussammlung Inv.-Nr. P. 11710.

29. *P.Berol. 11710, fragment a(→).* Staatliche Museen zu Berlin Preußischer Kulturbesitz, Papyrussammlung Inv.-Nr. P. 11710.

30. *P.Berol. 11710, fragment b(↓)*. Staatliche Museen zu Berlin Preußischer Kulturbesitz, Papyrussammlung Inv.-Nr. P. 11710.

31. *P.Berol. 11710, fragment b(→)*. Staatliche Museen zu Berlin Preußischer Kulturbesitz, Papyrussammlung Inv.-Nr. P. 11710.